FROM WELFARE TO WELLBEING
The future of social care

Edited by Liz Kendall and
Lisa Harker

30-32 Southampton Street, London WC2E 7RA
Tel: 020 7470 6100 Fax: 020 7470 6111
info@ippr.org.uk
www.ippr.org
Registered charity 800065

The Institute for Public Policy Research (ippr), established in 1988, is Britain's leading independent think tank on the centre left. The values that drive our work include delivering social justice, deepening democracy, increasing environmental sustainability and enhancing human rights. Through our well-researched and clearly argued policy analysis, our publications, our media events, our strong networks in government, academia and the corporate and voluntary sector, we play a vital role in maintaining the momentum of progressive thought.

ippr's aim is to bridge the political divide between the social democratic liberal and liberal traditions, the intellectual divide between the academics and the policy makers and the cultural divide between the policy-making establishment and the citizen. As an independent institute, we have the freedom to determine our research agenda. ippr has charitable status and is funded by a mixture of corporate, charitable, trade union and individual donations.

Research is ongoing, and new projects being developed, in a wide range of policy areas including sustainability, health and social care, social policy, citizenship and governance, education, economics, democracy and community, media and digital society and public private partnerships. We will shortly embark on major new projects in the fields of social justice, overseas development and democratic renewal. In 2003 we will be moving to new premises where we aim to grow into a permanent centre for contemporary progressive thought, recognised both at home and globally.

For further information you can contact ippr's external affairs department on info@ippr.org.uk, you can view our website at www.ippr.org and you can buy our books from central books on 0845 458 9911 or email ippr@centralbooks.com.

Trustees

Production & design by **EMPHASIS**
ISBN 1 86030 204 1
© IPPR 2002

Contents

Acknowledgments
About the contributors

1. A vision for social care   1
    Liz Kendall and Lisa Harker

2. Future drivers of change   22
    John McTernan

3. The future aims and objectives of social care   38
    Gerald Wistow

4. The workforce for social work and social care   68
    Liam Hughes

5. Structures and accountability   94
    Anne Davies

Acknowledgements

We would like to thank the Association of Directors of Social Services and Community Care magazine without whose generous support this book would not have been possible.

We are grateful to all those who participated in the series of seminars which discussed earlier drafts of the chapters in this book. In particular, we would like to thank Bob Welch and Caroline Abrahams for their comments and suggestions throughout the course of the project. However, the views expressed in the chapters remain the responsibility of the authors.

We would also like to thank Helena Scott from IPPR for her valuable help in producing this report.

About the authors

Anne Davies is an independent policy analyst. She has researched and written reports on issues of national and local governance for IPPR and the King's Fund health charity. Her recent publications include *Improving London's Health: the role of the Greater London Authority* (King's Fund 2000), *Developing Health Improvement Programmes* (King's Fund 1999) and *Voices off: Tackling the democratic deficit in health* (IPPR 1995). As a researcher at the Outer Circle Policy Unit, Anne produced reports on quangos, ministerial patronage and Commons' Select Committees.

Lisa Harker is Deputy Director at the Institute for Public Policy Research where she is responsible for overseeing IPPR's research programme and with the Director has oversight of the day-to-day management of the organisation. Her own research interests include tax and benefit policy, poverty, family policy and childcare. Until March 2000 Lisa was UK Advocacy Co-ordinator at Save the Children and previously worked for BBC News as a Social Affairs Specialist and as Campaigns Team Co-ordinator at Child Poverty Action Group. She is also Chair of Trustees at Daycare Trust and a former Executive Committee member of the Fabian Society.

Liam Hughes took up post as Chief Executive of East Leeds Primary Care Trust in January 2002, after six years as Strategic Director for Social Services and Community Development in Bradford and five years as Chief Social Services Officer in Kirklees. He worked in mental health resettlement in Lambeth and Community Care Services in Barnet. He has been a member of the Advisory Committee to the Children and Young People's Unit and is a Non-Executive Director of the Health Development Agency.

Liz Kendall is an Associate Director at IPPR and responsible for running the Institute's programme of research on health and social care. She was previously the Fellow of the Public Health Programme at the King's Fund. From 1996 to 1998, Liz was a Special Adviser to the Rt Hon Harriet Harman, MP, Secretary of State for Social Security and Minister for Women.

John McTernan is a columnist for *Scotland on Sunday* and one of Scotland's leading political thinkers. Specialising in strategic thinking, he is currently working with a range of public and private sector organisations across the UK. He was formerly Head of Strategy for the Scottish Executive and has worked at a senior level in the private and voluntary sectors.

Gerald Wistow is the Director of the Nuffield Institute for Health at the University of Leeds and he has also been the Chair of the PCT in Hartlepool since April 2001. Prior to taking up his appointment as Director of the Institute in 1997, he founded and led the Institute's Community Care Division and was appointed the University's first Professor of Health and Social Care in 1992.

1. A vision for social care
Liz Kendall and Lisa Harker

> In social work and social care we are currently in an in-between state, one of leaving the old but not yet having arrived in the new. It is a period of both anxiety and potential – and exactly the time to look ahead.

This assessment of social care's position at the beginning of the 21st century, identified by Liam Hughes' chapter in this book, is apposite. The winds of change generated by demographic, socio-cultural and technological forces are beginning to be felt across our public services. A more prosperous and informed population is demanding more personalised and convenient services, shaped around their needs. People are living longer and healthier lives, creating new patterns of retirement. The potential for new technology to reshape services and transform the relationships between users and providers has only just begun to be explored. Yet much of the landscape remains unchanged. Staff shortages continue to be a major problem. Structural change has become a permanent feature of the policy environment, with a never-ending search to find more effective institutions to deliver co-ordinated services. Poverty and social exclusion continue to blight too many of our communities, presenting major challenges for public services, despite the vast array of initiatives and increased investment emerging from central government.

This scene is familiar across the public services. Yet, in many ways, the challenges facing social care are distinct. Social care is not universally experienced or universally accessible like education or the NHS. It focuses on some of the most vulnerable and excluded people in society, with services including elements of both 'care' and 'control'. This can make the nature of the relationship between users and providers quite different from that of other public services.

Social care lacks the clear identity of other public services, partly for historical reasons. Social care is a relatively recent term: some of what is now called social care used to be considered health care. Social care is not embodied by a single type of service, institution or organisation. It includes local authority child protection services, residential care for the elderly provided in private homes, services for people with learning disabilities delivered by the voluntary sector, plus services from a range of new agencies like Sure Start, Connexions and the Children's Fund. This contrasts with health care where services are provided by an easily identifiable organisation – the NHS – with a clear focus: that of treating ill health (albeit to the continuing despair of the public health world). Social care in general, and social work in particular, also suffers from a lack of professional identity. Social work's emergence as a profession has been more tortured and contested than other professions, notably the medical establishment. This lack of institutional and professional identity contributes to the sense that social care is being driven by the agenda of others, especially the NHS.

There is much in the history of social care of which the sector can be proud. It has a track record of innovation and good practice, including user involvement and collaborative working, and has successfully delivered complex and often ground-breaking policy agendas such as care in the community. Yet at the same time, social care has lost its strategic focus. Services have been overly concerned with processes rather than outcomes, have tended to be been crisis-driven rather than preventive, and their mistakes have often been high profile, particularly in child protection.

All these factors have combined to produce a sector which seems to lack confidence and influence. The perception (and often reality) is that social care does not have a strong voice in national debates or contribute as much as it could to key policy initiatives on the ground. Whilst the Government has made clear its commitment to investing in and modernising public services, the focus is on the NHS, education, transport and crime. Social care is comparatively overlooked.

This book takes a step back from current debates in order to build a vision for social care in 2020. It focuses not on the future of social work or social services but on the future of the social care sector as a whole. In considering what role social care might have in decades to come it seeks to take account of the likely demographic and societal changes that lie ahead. But it does not seek to predict the future or provide a detailed blueprint for reform. Rather, it is hoped that this book will be thought-provoking and stimulate debate.

Its chapters build from first principles. John McTernan assesses what the needs and demands for social care are likely to be in ten to fifteen years time; Gerald Wistow explores the future aims and objectives of social care; Liam Hughes asks what kind of skills and workforce will be necessary; and Anne Davies outlines the structures and accountability mechanisms necessary to ensure effective delivery on the ground. What these chapters suggest is that the future of social care must be radically different from the reality being faced today. This will require a revolution in social care policy and the implementation of measures which go directly against the grain of key elements of current thinking within both government and the sector itself.

A universal service

Our vision for 2020 is that social care will meet universal needs and have universal support, even if its services are not universally experienced. We do believe that more people will have contact with social care by 2020, partly because of demographic changes but also because the focus of services should become more preventative and community-based. But at present, too many people aspire not to need social care. It is often perceived as providing poor services for the poor. Social care must become more universally understood and appreciated, particularly if it is to secure the sustained investment that it needs. This will require improvements to the quality of services and increased public understanding about both what social care is trying to achieve and what society's role is in the process.

The challenge of securing greater support for social care is not new. Social care has long sought to demonstrate that it benefits the whole community, not just those who use its services. As Gerald Wistow reminds us, the 1968 Seebohm Report (which led to the unification of children's and welfare services under the responsibility of local authority social service departments) argued that the whole community 'consumes the social services, whether directly or indirectly, as well as paying for them through taxation'. This view has been echoed by the current Government:

> Social services are for all of us...we all benefit if social services are providing good, effective services for those who need them

> ... Breakdowns in services for young offenders, homeless people or people with mental heath problems can have damaging consequences for other people as well as individuals themselves (Department of Health 1998).

Some public services such as health and education both meet universal needs and are universally used. Yet whilst social care matters universally not all aspects of it are used universally, nor would we want them to be. An important difference between social care and other public services is that it provides both 'care' and 'control'. Whilst many aspects of social care, such as residential care for older people or adoption services, are widely used, not everyone could or should use the 'control' element, for example child protection.

John McTernan argues that universal support for a service is not dependent on its universal use. He suggests that people do not need to use a service to believe it requires and deserves resources. The key to building support for services which are not universal is to ensure that when they are used, they are accessible, convenient and of the highest possible quality. This is one of the most important challenges facing social care over the coming years.

One of the main reasons why Seebohm argued for unified social service departments was the hope they would help tackle the belief that people who use social services are on the boundaries of acceptable society, and in turn help attract more resources. Yet such attitudes remain entrenched more than thirty years later, one reason why the role of children's services may need to be re-thought.

Anne Davies makes a persuasive case that if we want people to accept and value social care, they are more likely to do so if they have a sense of common ownership and mutual benefit: 'The authority which social care must have cannot depend on the force of law but is derived from its democratic legitimacy and its connectedness to the community it serves.' This, she suggests, is a strong argument in favour of local authorities remaining the appropriate framework of governance in which to deliver social care, although this must be seen in the context of wider debates about re-invigorating local democracy.

From welfare to wellbeing

Gerald Wistow notes that, although now over thirty years old, the Seebohm Report has a remarkably contemporary feel. Seebohm advocated services that would promote citizen's participation and consumer choice – both important themes of current government policy – and the creation of 'physical and social environments which people find it pleasant to live in', foreshadowing environmental and quality of life issues which have recently come to the fore. The report argued that the health and wellbeing of individuals cannot be improved without addressing the needs of the wider community, emphasising themes that are central to today's focus on tackling social exclusion. Seebohm called for services:

> To engage in the extremely difficult and complex task of encouraging and assisting the development of community identity and mutual aid, particularly in areas characterised by rapid population turnover, high delinquency, child deprivation and mental illness and other indices of social pathology (Report of the (Seebohm) Committee on Local Authority and Allied Personal Social Services, 1968).

Seebohm stressed that this would require 'the greatest possible number of individuals to act reciprocally, giving and receiving service for the wellbeing of the whole community'.

These issues are likely to be just as relevant in the years ahead. We live in an increasingly wealthy and prosperous society. New diagnostic medicines herald advances against previously untreatable diseases. People are living longer, healthier lives and have more opportunities for leisure and travel than ever before. Yet we are by no means a society at ease with itself. People feel increasingly pressurised as they spend less time at home with their families and more time at work or commuting. They feel they lack control over their work and their local environment, buffeted by changes taking place beyond their communities and even national boundaries. This contributes to a sense of disconnection from society and its decision-making processes.

Thus making a reality of Seebohm's basic aims and the values that underpin them is critical to our vision for social care in 2020. Social care's focus must be on empowering individuals to maximise their abilities and opportunities, to lead lives that are as independent and autonomous as possible, and to participate in lifestyles that are valued by their wider society. This vision can only be achieved within and through strong and empowered communities.

It also requires social care to play a central role in delivering quality of life and liveability agendas, shifting its framework from one essentially based on concepts of welfare to those of wellbeing. In the thirty years since the Seebohm Report was published, social care practitioners have struggled to deliver against ill defined and often conflicting social policy objectives with levels of resources which cannot readily be challenged because the product of social care has not itself been identified. In future, the state must define the level of wellbeing it is willing to underwrite through social care, over and above that provided by the basic Social Security net, and set clear boundaries of respective responsibilities. Creating mechanisms for discretion, for example allowing voters to opt to pay more taxes or higher charges at the local or regional level, will be important in managing public expectations of what it is reasonable for the state to provide in terms of social care and what individuals and their families are expected to provide for themselves.

Outcome oriented

Building services based on strong values will not be enough to win politicians' support in a climate where progress must be demonstrated under an increasingly sharp media spotlight. Social care's aims and values must be translated into clear outcomes that are tangible to the users and providers of services, the public who pays for and benefits from them, and to politicians who will ultimately be held accountable.

Yet social care, like many public services, has been poor at focusing on outcomes to date. Services have too often been dominated by concerns about processes and structures, not by what they are actually seeking to achieve. Our vision for 2020, therefore, is that social care is highly outcome oriented. This challenge which has already acknowledged through developments like Quality Protects, the National Service Framework for older people and the strategy of the Children and Young People Unit. However, outcome oriented services have yet to be adequately defined, let alone become a reality, across many parts of the system. Furthermore, ensuring social care delivers high quality outcomes means meeting users' needs in the round and recognising the interdependence of outcomes being sought at the individual and community level. This will in turn require a much greater focus on users and a significant shift away from crisis interventions towards a more preventive approach.

Holistic and interdependent

Social care must recognise the holistic nature of people's needs. Gerald Wistow cites the example of a safe discharge from hospital: from a purely medical perspective this is one that is clinically safe, in other words that the person is physically capable of moving back home. However a safe discharge from a non-clinical perspective would lead to the inclusion of broader community issues, such as whether the person has a safe home and environment to return to.

Outcomes must acknowledge people's emotional and psychological needs, not just their physical ones. Gerald Wistow outlines research which suggests that over a third of people living in the community five years after having survived a stroke suffer from depression. Between a third and a half of their carers also suffer from depression. Stroke care based on restricted definitions of need is therefore likely to lead to poor quality outcomes for individuals and their carers.

The research into stroke survivors also demonstrates that services which focus purely on delivering individual outcomes are likely to fail. Wistow argues that the ability of stroke survivors to live independently (an important overall objective of current Government policy) is clearly related to the quality and quantity of their inter-personal relationships and their engagement with family and social networks as providers of emotional and practical support. Thus independent living can only be realised in tandem with, and as an expression of, collective outcomes. The provision of holistic and interdependent social care implies new relationships between professionals, families and their communities. As a society we often duck the issue of where the responsibilities of professional care end and those of the individual, family or community begin. However a clearer understanding of these boundaries will be vital if public support for social care is to be maintained. Public expectations of what it is reasonable for the state to provide and what individuals and families should provide for themselves will ultimately shape the future of social care services and these expectations will need to be negotiated locally.

User focused

An explicit focus on users' needs is essential to delivering high quality outcomes. However, too many of our public services have been driven not by the needs of service users but by those of the institutions and professions that deliver them. Transforming this situation will be critical to retaining support for public services in future. IPPR's own research, for example, suggests that an important factor shaping people's perceptions of the quality of care they receive is the degree to which services are shaped to meet their individual needs (Edwards and Clarke 2001).

Social care has certainly been at the forefront of pioneering ways to tackle this problem, most notably through user-involvement. Yet, as Gerald Wistow argues, whilst user involvement has become more developed over the past twenty years, successive governments have failed to ensure it becomes rooted in everyday practices. New service developments like Sure Start have made user involvement central to their work. However, if user involvement is to be embedded across mainstream service provision, more effective incentives and mechanisms must be found, raising important challenges for the performance management of services and the role of regulatory bodies.

Demand for more user-focused services is likely to increase over the coming years. The ethos of services based on the welfare state of the 1940s – which John McTernan describes as 'Be patient, join the queue, wait your turn, be grateful its free' – is unsustainable in today's increasingly consumerist society.

However, there are limits to the consumer model for social care, as Gerald Wistow's discussion of the issue of choice illustrates. Users of some social care services, like child protection, do not choose to access them. Since access to social care is currently a relatively rare lifetime event, users lack the knowledge necessary to make informed choices. The model of social care we advocate here is also one that implies responsibilities as well as rights: a citizenship, rather than consumer, model.

Co-production – where producers and consumers collaborate to produce more personal and customised products – could play an important role in shaping public service provision over the coming years. Research suggests this could lead to better outcomes for individuals and society as a whole. For example, there is increasing evidence in the field of healthcare that giving users a greater role and supporting them to manage aspects of their care, particularly those with long term conditions, can lead to better outcomes, improved quality of life and a reduction in use of statutory service provision (Kendall 2001).

We need to start seeing people not just as recipients or consumers of services but also as a resource or co-producer of their own wellbeing and care. This means replacing paternalistic and dependent relationships with the notion of reciprocal care. Enabling people to give help as well as receive it, thereby demonstrating that they are themselves valuable, may be crucial to rebuilding connections in our increasingly factured and atomised society and particularly important in the light of future trends such as the increasing proportion of people living alone. It also means abandoning the consumerist approach to public service reform which dominates the current policy agenda and instead adopting a citizenship model, where rights to high quality, user-focused services are matched by appropriate roles and responsibilities for individuals and the wider community.

Preventive

The 2020 vision of social care delivering high quality, holistic outcomes implies a significant shift away from the last minute, crisis point interventions which all too often characterise today's service provision. Gerald Wistow notes that social care was born out of the vestiges of the Poor Laws and services which sought to 'tidy away' those considered on the fringes of normal life: the infirm, the mentally disturbed, older people who did not have the means for a dignified retirement and 'problem' families on the boundaries of society. Seebohm hoped that unified social service departments would promote the development of more preventive services thereby helping to end the Poor Law legacy and the socially divisive attitudes and practices which stemmed from it.

Yet social services still tend to focus on interventions with vulnerable groups, rather than on prevention. Liam Hughes describes the vicious circle where a lack of investment in preventive services has forced social work into reactive mode. The scope of social work has been narrowed to casework with an emphasis on assessment and care management rather than on providing direct therapeutic interventions. The fear of making mistakes and being publicly pilloried has reinforced this trend. Social work's narrowing skills base means that instead of seeking to re-connect individuals to their own resources and the resources of their family, friends and wider community, the primary response is to allocate statutory resources. These may be provided at levels which are initially appropriate but which are not then reduced as users needs decline. The consequence is that whilst in theory social services have sought to empower users they have in reality often created greater dependency. Although interest in Family Group Conferences and kinship care has increased recently, the wider community and groupwork approaches which are vital to empowering individuals and promoting wellbeing tend to be pursued through new services like Sure Start and Connexions, not social work.

More investment in preventive services, a greater focus on community involvement and a substantially enhanced role for the voluntary sector will all be vital over the coming years: factors Seebohm actually envisaged over thirty years ago. There is a particular need to address the gap in service provision for vulnerable groups, as opposed to those who are already in acute need, a fact that has been acknowledged through the development of services like Sure Start. However, universal services like education and health could also do much more to help identify those who would benefit from interventions at an earlier stage. Their failure to do so to date is partly due to the chronic under-investment in public services and the pressures of delivering major structural reforms under successive governments. However, it is also because schools and hospitals and the staff who work in them do not consider such work part of their core functions. Embedding the sense that these issues are everybody's responsibility – at the community and institutional level – is one of the most important challenges facing social care. Identifying the risk indicators that enable early intervention to be targeted appropriately and building consensus about them amongst the different agencies is a vital first step.

The 2002 Spending Review announced that each upper tier English Authority will be required to put in place systems for identifying, referring and tracking children at risk by April 2003. Whilst this move is welcome, the overwhelming focus of government policy remains on adults, not children (despite regular bouts of attention due to high profile child abuse cases) and presents a barrier to greater action on prevention. The extra money allocated to social services from this year's Comprehensive Spending Review, for example, is primarily going to older people. As ever, concerns about the NHS dominate: the need to free up beds occupied by older people in order to reduce waiting lists is of paramount political importance. The focus on older people is likely to become even stronger in future as the population ages and the demanding 'baby boomer' generation becomes the primary consumer of social care. This trend can already be seen across the Atlantic, where US seniors constitute one of the most powerful lobbies in American politics. Since older people are consistently more likely to vote than younger people, they will be a difficult constituency for politicians to ignore.

Yet a more appropriate balance between the policy priorities of children and adults must be found if services are to shift upstream. A fundamental obstacle to achieving this, however, is the huge challenge facing child protection which skews the focus of debate, drawing in attention and resources which are arguably vital but which ultimately help perpetuate the vicious circle we urgently need to break. This raises the question of whether some mechanism for separating child protection needs to be found in order to enable the rest of social care to shift its focus towards empowering vulnerable people, mobilising communities and promoting wellbeing and prevention.

Implications for the workforce

Our 2020 vision will mean transforming the roles of those working in social care. The continued existence of separate professions working closely with the same service groups presents a major barrier to delivering more user-focused services. Liam Hughes argues that a major realignment of professional boundaries will be required in future and ultimately the creation of new professions. For example, a new profession combining youth and community work, social work, adolescent mental health services and careers services could emerge to provide more holistic services for young people. Elements of nursing, occupational therapy, social work and home support could be drawn together under a new profession focusing on intermediate care for older people.

The seeds of these new professions have already been planted, through joint courses in nursing and social work and in new agencies like Connexions. They are being driven partly by the recognition that models of service provision based on society as it was in the 1940s – where the concept of teenager did not exist and where there were much shorter periods of retirement – are no longer appropriate. Continuing staff shortages across related areas of public services will create further momentum for more joined-up professions to emerge.

This vision means that by 2020, social work as we currently know it will cease to exist, although its values will remain integral to the development of new professions. It goes against the grain of current government policy which is seeking to strengthen social work, for example through the introduction of a three-year degree-level qualification. It also implies major changes in the training of the future social care workforce, with the current emphasis on generic skills and practice being replaced by a more specialised focus around age related groups. Again, staff shortages are likely to re-enforce this trend. Growing recruitment difficulties in social care are already prompting major re-evaluations of skills mix which are likely to result in an increasing proportion of vocationally qualified staff and a decreasing proportion of professionally qualified staff. This suggests that in future, we may see the emergence of social care administrators for some user groups assessing needs and co-ordinating services for most users, and referring those with more complex needs on to a smaller number of highly specialised practitioners.

Whilst some will view this agenda as threatening, it will be crucial to ensuring those working in social care take their rightful place in the development of wider policy agendas. As Liam Hughes points out:

> Given the experience of social workers in poor neighbourhoods and Seebohm's aspirations for comprehensive community services, why hasn't social work as a profession been more central to the fight to overcome social exclusion and to regenerating local communities? Some Social Services Departments have been actively involved...but the impression is that social work has been seen by government as part of the problem rather than the solution.

In transforming the roles of those working with the profession, it will be necessary to ensure that the vision and values of the social care workforce are shared. Some element of core training for a wide range of specialist professions may still be required. The balance between generic and specialist training will need to tilt towards greater specialisation but not at the cost of dismantling the very notion of the social care professional. Above all, it is vital that the new professions adopt an evidence-based approach to ensure they evaluate their performance and learn from their mistakes. The establishment of the Social Care Institute for Excellence provides an important starting point for developing such an approach.

Structures and accountability

The social care services of the future must be more accountable to the public. Anne Davies reminds us that public services like social care – which are authorised in statute and publicly funded – must be held accountable in order to assess competence, ensure financial probity, safeguard administrative propriety and guarantee responsiveness. Genuine accountability exists when those to whom an account is given can exercise direct sanctions over those who are accountable:

> The traditional way of achieving public accountability is through democracy, which obtains a mandate for public action through periodic elections. However flawed this may be, no better alternative has been found. A variety of measures can be used to augment democracy, such as public consultations, scrutiny rights and the involvement of user groups, but they cannot in themselves provide an adequate substitute.

The future accountability of social care must be seen as part of wider debates about strengthening local democracy. Finding the appropriate balance between central and local responsibility for public service provision is a challenge which has yet to be satisfactorily solved. It often seems as if the current impasse suits all sides. National politicians can blame local government for failing to deliver when things go wrong and local councillors can blame Whitehall for refusing to provide sufficient resources or for stifling innovation. Yet it is the users of services and the wider public that ultimately suffer from this stalemate. The lack of connectedness that results – the public's sense that they cannot affect change over the services that matter most to them – may be a critical factor in the declining participation rates in local and national elections that should be of huge concern to us all.

Debates about the future of social care cannot, therefore, be separated from questions about the future of local government and its relationship with other levels of government, which in turn cannot be divorced from the need to increase public participation in the democratic process. There is currently a mismatch between the social care policy imperatives of empowering, enabling and including and the structures of local government which can often be disabling and excluding. Re-invigorating our democracy ultimately means convincing the public that their views and votes count. A detailed analysis of how this can be achieved is beyond the scope of this book. However, it may include a new voting system based on proportional representation, new voting methods such as postal votes, and new ways of involving the public beyond the ballot box such as citizens' panels, citizens' juries and other deliberative techniques. These changes must go hand in hand with strengthened local accountability for the services which matter most to people, including health and social care. Greater control over the resources for these services, for example through increased local tax raising powers, is likely to be an important element of this process.

Adult services

Social care needs to remain within the accountability framework provided by local government (albeit highly re-invigorated). An important theme of our 2020 vision for social care is that its structures should flow from the outcomes it is seeking to achieve suggesting a move towards more age-related organisations. This has not been the case hitherto: rather it has been the nature of the relationship between health and social care that has dominated debates about how social care should be organised. Anne Davies argues that this must end: 'Social services departments face pressure for joint working not only from the NHS but from a wide range of other agencies. Its ability to do this will be impaired if its structure is dictated solely by the demands of the NHS.'

The current Government's preferred model of ensuring more effective working across health and social care is that of Care Trusts. Supporters claim Care Trusts will ensure more effective services focused on users' needs. Opponents fear that an holistic view of users needs will be lost in the predominantly medical culture of the NHS. Anne Davies reminds us that there can be trade-offs between the accountability and effectiveness of a public service. Care Trusts may offer one way forward, at a cost to democratic accountability, if they can demonstrably provide a solution to the NHS/social care interface problem where other structures have failed. Yet the evidence on this point is far from clear. Only one Care Trust has been the subject of research to date. The results are not encouraging, suggesting the new arrangements have failed to produce significant benefits to users during the first two years. This echoes the evidence Gerald Wistow cites from Northern Ireland which suggests that the fundamental barriers to delivering more joined-up services may be as much about professional values as about structures (Report of the Royal Commission on the National Health Service 1978; McCoy 2000). In the absence of sufficient evidence, and in the context of the threat they place to delivering holistic services, Care Trusts should not be rolled out across the country.

An alternative way of dealing with NHS/social care boundary problems would be to integrate health and social care responsibilities in a way that ensures both are locally accountable. This would mean accentuating the distinction between commissioning and providing services, which goes against the prevailing climate in health policy. Anne Davies envisages a scenario for 2020 where local government is responsible for commissioning health and social care (something Gerald Wistow also supports). The NHS (along with a range of voluntary and private organisations) provides health services but no longer commissions primary care services from itself. Primary Care Trusts are dis-aggregated into smaller provider trusts, operating on contracts with the local authority. Such a vision is attractive in that it allows for both greater accountability and more co-ordination in health and social care services.

Both Anne Davies and Gerald Wistow also raise the possibility of some strategic responsibilities for health and social care taking place at the regional level. The costs and benefits of creating a regional tier of government are beyond the scope of this book. However, regional level developments are already emerging in some parts of the country. For example a pan-London Child Protection Committee is being established to help develop more coherent working across the capital. The development of regional government will have important consequences for health and social care services and further work is needed to assess the implications of this process in future.

Children's services

Whilst debates about the structure of social care have so far been dominated by its relationship with the NHS, the future of children's services has recently come to the fore, mainly as a result of the inquiry into the death of Victoria Climbié.

The results of the cross cutting review on 'children at risk' in the 2002 Spending Review made clear the Government's belief in the case for structural change to ensure the better co-ordination of children's services. The Review announced that Children's Trusts, which will unify the various agencies involved in providing services to children at the local level, will be piloted. Although plans are at an early stage, it is thought that Children's Trusts will contain services provided by local authorities, the NHS, and possibly other bodies, and build on existing arrangements such as Health Act flexibilities.

Anne Davies explores how such an approach might be developed within the democratic accountability of local government. She cites the example of Hertfordshire County Council, which has amalgamated its Education Department with Social Services to form a Children, Schools and Families Department. Children's services, including child protection, have merged with education, the youth offending team and youth services, all of whom work to a unified management. Liam Hughes suggests that in future, integrated children and families services might also incorporate community health services and child and adolescent mental health services. This approach is supported by the Local Government Association, the Association of Directors of Social Services and the NHS Confederation. They propose a model that would build on the Children's Strategic Partnership Boards being established to improve planning for vulnerable children to include all children, within the overall framework of Local Strategic Partnerships and the accountability of local government (LGA, ADSS and NHS Confederation, 2002).

This integrated model of service provision, within the accountability framework of local government, is integral to our 2020 vision. However, there are strong reasons to consider creating a separate service focussing specifically on child protection. Seamless multi-agency working may only be possible through the creation of a new service dedicated to safeguarding children. This could help ensure that child protection becomes the responsibility of all the relevant agencies, rather than solely that of social services. It would emphasise the specialist skills and expertise required to safeguard children. It could also help remove families' uncertainties about whether social services are investigating them or supporting them, which can be a barrier to both effective working with families and to building wider public support for social care as a whole. It is important to consider the creation of such a service within the context of our overall vision for social care, which sees enhanced local control over services including greater responsibility for their resourcing through local taxation. Local ownership of child protection services will still be vital. But since local variation in services would be considered unacceptable, there is a role for a national body which would oversee standards and enable lessons to be shared.

Those who oppose a separate child protection service argue that childrens' families' needs are holistic and cannot be broken up in such a simplistic manner. They also claim that separation would reinforce beliefs that child protection services are for people on the margins of society, thus increasing the danger that they have insufficient support and resources and remain poor services for the poor. Yet separating the 'control' element of childrens' services may be a crucial step in enabling the rest of social care to deliver the empowering and enabling agenda. This suggestion raises a number of issues which require fuller investigation, including the appropriate balance between local and national responsibilities. It would also be necessary to ensure those working in such an agency avoid 'burn out' and retain their skills to deliver more empowering and enabling services through a system of secondment or rotation.

In addition, it must be stressed that structural reform does not provide a panacea. The evidence submitted to the Laming inquiry into the death of Victoria Climbié, for example, suggests a wide range of factors had a role to play including the pay, skills, experience and career structure of staff working in child protection and the ways of working of other services like the NHS. Structural reform alone will not prevent such terrible tragedies happening again.

Delivering change

Changing cultures and attitudes

Indeed, the obsession with institutional reform has been a persistent weakness in social care policy making to date. It is often much easier to change the structure of public services than their culture, particularly for governments who need to demonstrate progress during the course an electoral cycle. Of course institutions play their part in determining the culture of service provision, but this alone will be insufficient to deliver genuine change. Policy needs to pay far more attention to implementation capacities in local services, suggesting that the route to better outcomes is through integrated pathways organised around evidence-based protocols which specify the roles, responsibilities and sequence of interventions by the different professionals involved.

Gerald Wistow also emphasises that genuinely transforming services to meet needs will require fundamental changes in the attitudes of providers and service users alike. He cites the experience of the 'Ordinary Life' initiative in the 1980s, which sought to implement the principle of normalisation (the right to a life as close to the normal as possible) for people with learning disabilities, as a case in point. Whilst attitudes towards people with learning disabilities have changed, the extent of discrimination that still exists amongst both providers and members of the public should not be underestimated. The values and principles of the Ordinary Life initiative have still to be universalised, despite considerable political and financial commitment. This is not an isolated case: recent research has revealed services discriminate against a range of other users, including black and minority ethnic users and older people.

Political leadership

Our vision for social care in 2020 raises important questions about the future role of politicians. There are now regular calls for politicians to focus more on setting long term objectives for public services and less on their day to day management. However, as John McTernan points out, the precise opposite is happening in today's post ideological world. This creates a major problems since politicians are often extremely poor managers. This is not simply because they lack experience:

> The political skill set is very different from the managerial one and for good reason: politicians do a different job. At their best they mediate complex policy issues in understandable ways to widely varying audiences, they assemble coalitions for change, they argue for, and make, trade-offs... [These skills are] much needed in our world with its combination of complex risks, mistrusts of traditional authority and instantaneous 24-hour communication. Yet politicians feel compelled to ignore these skills in favour of entering a world of implementation where at best they add little and at worst they import the command and control style which suits running a political movement but not the running of personal services.

John McTernan explores the impact of politicians' obsession with the media, which has lead to a fondness for announcing eye catching initiatives. This works against the guiding mantra of managerial politics, 'what matters is what works', since such initiatives are rarely based on the evidence. The danger is that the interventionist approach adopted by many of today's pragmatic politicians not only fails to deliver real change but also ends up re-enforcing public cynicism and disengagement with the political process as a whole. The answer is for politicians is to pull back from micro-managing public services and instead focus on setting strategic goals, based on clearly articulated values and principles around which they seek to build support.

However, as Anne Davies points out, this would require the Government to be far less concerned about the so-called 'post-code lottery' of care. One of the main reasons for decentralising and devolving power is to give people the freedom to do things differently. This will inevitably lead to variation, something politicians and the public have shied away from in the past. Debates about which variations might be considered acceptable and which unacceptable have not had the same prominence as calls for an end to Whitehall control and for more power to be given to the front line. Yet such debates are vital if the rhetoric of decentralisation is to become a reality, and if public support is to be built throughout the process. This reinforces the case for keeping services within the framework of local democratic accountability.

Conclusion

Our vision for social care in 2020 is that it will seek to promote wellbeing by empowering individuals and their communities. The sector will provide high quality, outcome oriented services that are universally used by those who need them, while also being universally supported by those who do not. The predominant focus will be on delivering holistic, preventive services for vulnerable groups with highly specialised and targeted interventions for those in need.

Our vision is based on a model of social citizenship, where rights to high quality user-focused services are matched by individuals and communities taking on appropriate roles and responsibilities. It suggests that the core aims and values of social care identified by Seebohm will be as integral to people's needs over the next thirty years as they have been during the last. By finally making these values a reality, the sector will itself be empowered to play a leading and confident role in strategic policy development and future public service reform.

This vision will require fundamental changes to the roles of politicians, practitioners, users and the wider public. Central government's relationship with local government must be transformed through greater devolution of control and resources. Its relationship with social care and the NHS must also be radically rethought. Social work as we currently know it will cease to exist. Instead, new professions must emerge around key groups accompanied by greater specialisation. Social Services Departments will also disappear, replaced by age-related organisations held accountable to local government and a dedicated child protection service held accountable to national government. The strengthening of local democracy and the re-invigoration of public participation in democratic processes is implicit to this process.

The challenges our vision presents should not be underestimated, but neither should the prize: a world where individuals are valued in their own right, empowered to meet their full potential and enabled to participate and contribute to a more socially just and tolerant society. This is world social care can and must win.

Bibliography

Department of Health (1998) *Modernising Social Services* Cm 4169 London: The Stationery Office

Edwards L and Clarke R (2001) *Quality and the NHS: the Patient Perspective* London: IPPR (unpublished)

Kendall L (2001) *The Future Patient* London: IPPR

LGA, ADSS and NHS Confederation (2002) *Serving children well: a new vision for children's services* London: LGA

McCoy K (2000) *Review of Care in the Community* Social Services Inspectorate, Department of Health, Social Services and Public Safety, Northern Ireland

Report of the Royal Commission on the National Health Service (1978) Research Paper No 1, London: HMSO

Report of the (Seebohm) Committee on Local Authority and Allied Personal Social Services (1968) Cmnd 3703, London: HSMO

2. Future drivers of change
John McTernan

Social Service Departments have served the country well for over 30 years. Though often the most parodied and pilloried part of the public service, social workers have not just delivered the services envisaged by Seebohm but at times demonstrated an exemplary record in service innovation. User-led services and collaborative working are just a few examples. Alongside this record has been the undoubted success of implementing major changes in institutional structure and in practice following the landmark legislation of the 1980s: the NHS and Community Care Acts and the Children Act.

In many ways the election of the new Labour government in 1997 with its commitment to social inclusion, evidence based policy, joined up implementation and community based initiatives should have ushered in a new era for social work. Yet somehow it has been left behind. Education, education, education was at least the rhetorical priority. The New Deal and an elaborate system of tax credits occupied the intellects of the Chancellor and his closest allies. Now the National Health Service has won the public spending lottery. In contrast, social services' leaders and practitioners have struggled to impact on even those parts of the social policy agenda where they have the greatest expertise. Is this just a continuation of an underlying prejudice against the profession? Or are more deep-seated changes to user needs and demands underway which will ultimately reshape social care, its practices and its institutions?

This chapter seeks to examine the political, social and demographic forces which are driving change across the public sector, including social care.

Defining social care

Any attempt to define a vision for social care over the next ten to fifteen years time cannot simply focus on the future of Social Services Departments. If social care is to start setting its own agenda it must be seen free of its own institutional frameworks and instead develop its own conceptual framework. Only in this way can it avoid being seen merely as an adjunct to other public services, notably the NHS.

This raises the difficult question of definition. Social care is a relatively recent term: a formulation of the last thirty years. During this time, its boundaries have been fluid: some of what is now called social care used to be considered health care. Social care covers a range of areas and is not embodied by a single type of service, institution or organisation. It covers residential care for the elderly in private homes, services for people with learning disabilities provided by the voluntary sector, local authority child protection services and new services like Sure Start.

Values and principles

The contrast with health care appears stark. Health services are provided by an easily identifiable, nationally accessible organisation – the NHS – and have a clear focus: the treatment of ill health. Closer examination of the NHS does identify a more complex institutional settlement yet all the players in the NHS are united by a common value base. The Government has recently begun to argue that the NHS should be seen as a set of values and principles rather than as a specific institution: that what matters is that health care is delivered according to NHS principles (universally available, free at the point of use, based on need not ability to pay) not who delivers it. Underpinning this argument is a wish to open up the provision of healthcare to a greater diversity of providers from the public, private and voluntary sectors.

Social care is already delivered by just such a plurality of providers, so perhaps it should learn from health and seek to define itself by its values and principles. Those who work in social care already tend to define themselves by their values rather than their roles and responsibilities. A key challenge is to more clearly define these values and to build a consensus about them amongst policy makers, practitioners, opinion formers and the public. The core values of social care can often be straightforwardly articulated: respect for individual dignity, striving to provide independence and autonomy and protecting confidentiality. However, these need to be rooted in a broader framework. It is likely that the right model will be based on the concept of wellbeing rather than welfare. Perhaps the right starting point is the public health debate. The links between social care and health care are well known. There are strong connections between environmental factors, such as housing and needs for social care, as well as broader issues like transport and education (which are in turn related to issues like employability). Framed in this way it may be possible for social care to gain the wider support necessary to secure the additional resources it needs to invest in meeting demand.

However, clear values are not a 'get out of jail free' card in a world where politicians control resource allocation. Politics has its own practices and values which can clash harshly with those of people working in public services. Turning again to the health service, the overriding principle of health care since Hippocrates has been 'first do no harm'. You will search long and far for the politician who would sign up to this principle for themselves. 'Ready, Fire, Aim' is more often their motto.

Universal or targeted?

In addition to clear values it has been argued that social care services must become more universally available if they are to secure greater 'buy in' from the public at large. It is not at all clear that this is a solution. Social care contains a combination of 'care and control' services. Very few are pleased to need 'control' services. Most people want to avoid entanglement, often for good reason. As one mother observed: 'Trying to get your child out of care is like trying to get a stick off a rottweiler'. Those who receive 'care' services are increasingly demanding a tailored and personalised service rather than a universalist one. Where social care impacts on the growing middle classes – adoption, mental health, learning disabilities, residential care – we see pressure for consumerist provision.

The pursuit of universalist support through universalist provision is almost certainly a Snark hunt. It is not necessary to use the armed forces or the fire service, to believe they need and deserve resources. As with all service industries, the trick for social care is to provide the right services to the highest standards at the right time to the right people. This is, naturally, easier stated than delivered. Social care is aiming at not just a moving but an evolving target in social, political and demographic terms.

Social change

Affluence and education

The period since the Seebohm Report of 1968 has seen profound social change in British society. Living standards doubled between 1950 and 1975 and have doubled again between 1975 and 2000. Paralleling this increasing prosperity has been a huge increase in educational attainment. The proportion of young people attending university has risen from five per cent in the 1950s to over a third, and the government wants to see the proportion rise to 50 per cent or more in future. A small minority of those who do not go on to higher education leave school at 16. Education and affluence are dissolving social hierarchy and destroying deference. Money and time are liberating individuals to forge hugely varied patterns of leisure activity with the consequence that participation in mass activities, whether church-going, attending football matches or political campaigning, are in decline.

Decline in deference

All public services are being buffeted by this change. An educated, articulate public is impatient with the quality of services they receive. The 1940s wartime ethos of 'Be patient, join the queue, wait your turn, be grateful it's free' which pervades the traditional institutions of the welfare state is no longer accepted. People see transactions with the state in terms of rights (their own) not in terms of favours or charity (done to them). A wide range of 'intermediary' figures who in the past have drawn authority from the state, ranging from caretakers on estates to teachers and elected councillors, have fallen significantly in status. Their words, their actions, their instructions no longer go unchallenged.

Deference to authority was often in the past expressed in terms of trust. There has been a substantial shift away from traditional patterns of 'trust'. This has been driven in no small part by changing patterns of education. As important as the increase in access to higher education has been the increase in the people who in the United States would say they have had 'some college' (people who have participated in post-16 education without substantially increasing their formal educational qualifications). The result is the creation of a credulous public to parallel the formally educated public. The ensuing polarisation is visible in any high street bookshop. There has never been such a boom time for high quality, intellectually stretching popular science and every bookshop now features shelves of such work. However, these same shops have equal numbers of books devoted to complementary and alternative therapies. As GK Chesterton said, when people stop believing in God they don't believe in nothing, they believe in anything. 'Some education' is probably the single biggest contributor to that strange coalition of lower middle-class Daily Mail readers and post-modern, downwardly mobile, Bohemian middle-class Guardian readers who believe that the MMR vaccine is the devil's own creation.

Disintermediation

The information revolution is compounding these changes. On the one hand, cranks and obsessives can find any amount of 'evidence' through the Internet to back up their concerned campaigning or worrying. Un-refereed journals and unreliable sources abound. On the other, Information and Communication Technology is a revolutionary force, re-configuring organisations, services and relationships. In particular, the Internet presents the challenge of 'disintermediation': the ability of users to trade directly with providers of services which is dissolving the position of intermediaries. This process has started with insurance brokers, banks and travel agents but is moving rapidly into the public services: doctors, local authority employees and councillors (for who is more of an intermediary than a politician?).

This unravelling has barely begun. Authority is increasingly only lent temporarily by electors and local communities to politicians on condition that the politicians do not abuse their positions to disrupt the voters' lives. When the wrong judgement is made on a school or hospital closure local officials, appointed or elected, again and again find themselves out-organised. Now and again the contours of a new world are visible. The fuel duty protest was the first but by no means the last uprising against government organised with the aid of ICT, through mobile phones and the Internet. Just as Hartlepool's election of the monkey H'Angus as Mayor is only the beginning of the promotion of anti-Establishment maverick candidates to replace a failing political class.

Consumerism

The public are no longer approaching relationships with the state as captive clients but as active consumers. Public services and public officials (including politicians) have to offer a transactional value. They are also judged by the standards of the best private sector services. Accessibility is benchmarked against those areas, such as financial services, which have responded to the rise of the 24/7 lifestyle. Customer care is compared to the high standards experienced in leisure time spent at home and, increasingly, abroad. This trend towards consumerist attitudes is uncomfortable. It is sometimes resisted and even condemned as inappropriate by politicians and bureaucrats alike, but it is irreversible. Control over time plays an important role in quality of life as households find they are spending more time working and less time at home. Being able to access a service on their own terms becomes doubly important for people who are 'work rich/time poor'.

Choice

Can social care be customised to fit individual lifestyles? Those wedded to current patters of service provision will always attempt to defend their right to continue doing things as they have always done, often claiming that more personalised services will inevitably drive up costs. This is only true if you believe current patterns of provision must be taken as given: that costs of capital assets are staff are fixed and that innovation can only come 'on top'. Standardised services are not cheaper – they are just easier to deliver from the perspective of providers. They are also more easily audited in a tick-box fashion. Consumers prefer a personal approach because they would like a personal outcome. Where control has been put in the hands of users, we find that people would rather sell day centres and reshape staffing patterns to provide flexible, personal support than to be bussed to where the council and staff believe their needs are best served.

Some working in social care are reluctant to see the users of services as 'clients' or 'customers'. The role of the cash nexus here is a vexed one. There is no doubt that paying shifts the balance of power towards the consumer (though it does not always feel like that when dealing with a plumber or a garage). But it is perhaps a more subtle influence than a crude market-oriented analysis might imply. A critical development in modern consumer products is the movement towards co-production, where producers and consumer collaborate. Henry Ford may have said 'Any colour as long as it is black' but nowadays the car you purchase can be customized well beyond its colour and internal accessories, and the Dell computer you buy is built for you. If you shop at IKEA you literally co-produce your furniture: not fun when you open that flat-pack but a choice millions make because of cost and flexibility. It may be that re-conceptualising our public services, by putting co-production at the core, would be as powerful as re-organisating them.

This may also be a route through the most difficult of paradoxes: universal services fail the poorest but services for the poor are poor services. Reframed as services with and services by, rather than services to, we should have the ability to start seeing people not just as recipients or consumers of services but also as a resource, or 'co-producers' of their wellbeing and care.

Changing family structures

Family structures and formations have changed irreversibly, and undoubtedly this change has been fuelled by the same forces which underpin the rise of consumerism. Women's increasing access firstly to the workplace, and through education to professional employment, has been a significant contributor to rising household incomes. Independent access to money has eroded the traditional hierarchy and deference within the home and the increase in relationship breakdown and divorce is the ineluctable consequence. Liberation has meant just that for many women, though it continues to be lamented Canute-like by politicians of all parties. The traditional 1950s family model with one male breadwinner and a full-time housewife at home looking after the children is now only present in 11 per cent of households. A range of other family models flourish – many with both parents working, some with step-parents, others where separated adults share care for their children.

The general liberalising of social attitudes which started in the 1960s has spread through all classes and has had a direct and indirect impact on social services. For instance, the welcome end of the stigma against children being born outside marriage, the rise of lone parent families, ready access to reliable and effective contraception and abortion law reform have all contributed to the fall in adoption rates from around 20,000 a year in 1970 to 2,000 a year now.

The traditional welfare state based on the model of a 1940s/1950s lifestyle and lifecycle has struggled to accommodate these changes. Childcare has become a key component of the lives of almost all working families. Demands for its increased provision are being phrased in quite traditional universalist language, though the favoured policy option is demand side subsidy rather then supply side provision. Yet despite the efforts of the current Government, most parts of the country are a long way away from delivering the seamless, affordable and quality local services most parents want.

With all these changes it remains true that families, particularly extended families, remain a significant resource for social care, providing informal support, offering a sounding-board for complex decision-making around care options and playing a major role in socialisation and ultimately control. Yet these roles are rarely give the attention or support they deserve.

Race

Over the last forty years, the United Kingdom has been strengthened by its increasing diversity. Our black and Asian populations have driven economic growth in urban centres across England and, despite the offensive and ignorant observations of some mainstream politicians, we see integration and participation across the board: from families, where one in three children in black families are mixed race, through music, to sport, where almost fifty percent of the England football team are now black. One of social care's emerging challenges is how to provide appropriate services for an increasing number of black elders. Another, equally important challenge is to tackle the employment gap where young black and Asian men are disproportionately likely to be under-qualified and unemployed.

Networks

Current patterns of delivery in our public services are wedded to a geographical notion of identity. However, for many people geography is of questionable importance, since where they live is the least important definition of who they are, what they need and what they aspire to be. Freed from traditional mass 'industrial' activities, individuals have become captains of their own destiny. They live, work, learn and play through different networks with separate members and alignments. Geography has merit as the basis for organising street sweeping but it is limited in its application to personal services.

Political change

These social changes drive broader political change. Voters too have become consumers, no longer owned by political parties for life because of the way their parents voted. This is an entirely pragmatic response to the post ideological phase of politics we currently inhabit in which Blair and Major, Bush and Clinton, Chirac and Jospin are often hard in practice to distinguish. In the long run, centrist, managerialist politics may well feed the extremes of politics as voters look to outsiders to overthrow the establishment, but for the moment it is the only game in town. There are certain key characteristics to the current political climate.

Moral authoritarianism

There is a new moralistic and, at times, authoritarian tone. From the outset, the Labour government has articulated a new language of rights and responsibilities in its approach to social policy. Political slogans such as 'Work is the best form of welfare for people of working age', 'Welfare should be a safety net not a hammock' and 'There is no fifth option of a life on benefit' are firmly rooted in a view that there are no rights in society without reciprocal responsibilities. This position is certainly arguable philosophically. It also makes for powerful politics, and has emerged from a policy consensus that runs from American Conservatives like the former Governor of Wisconsin, Tommy Thompson, through to such genuinely radical British politicians as Peter Lilley, Frank Field and the Chancellor Gordon Brown.

The rights and responsibilities approach has also been applied to the reform of the criminal justice system. Arguably, this has been a success in the reshaping of the probation service. On the other hand, it has failed to have much purchase when applied to youth crime in general where it has generated policy initiatives later apologetically explained as 'metaphors'. In the race to chase perceived public opinion normally rational politicians (north and south of the border) end up sounding like King Lear – both portentous and empty:

> I will have such revenges on you both
> That all the world shall – I will do such things –
> What they are, yet I know not; but they shall be
> The terrors of the earth.

This is because instinct often trumps analysis and drives out another core component of managerialist politics: attention to the evidence.

Evidence based policy

The success of the New Deal is not solely down to the work of the Chancellor and his advisers, nor an outburst of creativity in the Departments of Social Security and Education and Employment. There has been over 30 years of research into welfare to work schemes and the lessons of success and failure have been built into later programmes. In contrast, for all the tough rhetoric about 'three strikes and you're out' the most successful anti-youth crime policy in the United States is floodlit, night-time basketball courts: honest, straightforward competitive diversion for teenage energy and aggression.

If what matters is what works then surely what is needed is switched-on public service management. But if that's right, what is the role for the politician? This tension is at the core of the philosophy of pragmatic politics.

Initiatives and targets

The current tenor of new Labour policy making is one of letting go, yet holding on at the same time. There is genuine commitment to gathering evidence and encouraging innovation to flourish from the bottom up, but this is accompanied by a torrent of targets, guidance and monitoring. The consequence is that some community based groups are finding it easier to find private sector partners for innovation than to have to go through the accountability processes demanded by government, whilst elsewhere funds go unspent.

At the same time politicians continue to feel that to be is to do, that if they are not in the papers they do not exist. Approaches are adopted in order to be eye-catching with scant attention to their evidential basis. Take the belief in faith based provision of welfare. On both sides of the Atlantic, politicians suggest religious schools and church based charities should play a critical role. This really is a genuine leap of faith. In other areas of service delivery, all parties suggest voluntary organisations offer added value: with no unions and lower unit costs to please the right, and no profit or shareholders to gratify the left.

Delivery

Managerialism in politics justifies itself with reference to delivery. Unfortunately, the choice of term illuminates a key weakness in modern political thinking. Delivery is what is done to white consumer goods by John Lewis. What goes on in our public services (or any human service) is very different. It has been said that politicians think making an announcement is 'delivering' whilst civil servants think it means issuing a circular. In reality, success actually rests on operations. However, operational management is not 'sexy' like policy making. If it was we would be overwhelmed by do-tanks and implementation wonks rather than think-tanks and policy wonks.

There is a fundamental problem here. Most politicians are extremely poor managers, as they have never had experience of managing anything before. In fact one could go further and argue that the political skill set is very different from the managerial one and for good reason: politicians do a different job. At their best, they mediate complex policy issues in understandable ways to widely varying audiences, they assemble coalitions for change, they argue for, and make, trade-offs and they are often intuitively responsive to broad shifts in public sentiment. A pretty broad set of skills that are much needed in our world with its combination of complex risks (like GMOs and MMR), mistrust of traditional authority and instantaneous 24-hour communication. Yet politicians feel compelled to ignore these skills in favour of entering the world of implementation where at best they add little, and at worst they import the command and control style which suits running a political movement but not the running of personal services.

This interventionist approach and its subsequent failure to deliver change may end up re-enforcing cynicism and disengagement with the political process, which is even more acute at the local than national level. This presents a major challenge to social services since they are based in local government. The solution is almost certainly for politicians to focus on setting broad aims and objectives for services rather than seeking to micro-manage them. Where consumer choice can discipline providers and help to drive up quality it should be allowed to create pressure. In other areas inspection should be used to ensure national minimum standards of service.

This is broadly the approach being taken in health by the current Secretary of State, Alan Milburn, but it is applicable across the public services. It ultimately requires central Government to be far less concerned about the so-called 'post-code lottery' of care. The very reason for decentralising and devolving power is to give people the freedom to do things differently. This will inevitably lead to some variation, but so long as there is public support for the values of social care and commitment to making these values a reality on the ground, variation may become more acceptable in future. Indeed local variety could lead to the public re-investing in local politics. It may seem hard to expect politicians to relinquish power, however it is the illusion of power they currently have: there is no megaphone loud enough, no cattle prod powerful enough, for a minister in Whitehall to affect the performance of a classroom teacher in Camberwell, let alone in Carlisle.

Demographic change

Britain, like the rest of Europe, is undergoing a profound demographic change. The population is ageing. This is a long slow change and much of it has happened already: there has been a larger increase in the elderly population in the last twenty years than there will be in the next twenty. But we will be passing some important symbolic milestones. In 2000, there were nearly 1.3 million more children aged under 16 than people of state pensionable age. However from 2007, the population of state pensionable age is projected to be greater than the number of children and by 2025 is projected to exceed it by nearly two million. (The speed of increase is slightly dampened by the increase in state pensionable age for women from 60 to 65 from 2010-2030.) Accompanying this shift in the balance of the population is an increase in life expectancy, which is projected to rise from 75.5 years in 2000 to 78.9 years in 2025 for men and from 80.3 years to 83.2 years for women.

These are the fundamental facts underlying pensions policy, approaches to long-term care and the question of long term financing of the National Health Service. The policy questions that arise from these changes have been explored by Lord Sutherland and the Royal Commission on Long Term Care and Derek Wanless in his report for the Treasury. How healthy and active will older people be and for how long? Does longer life mean longer dependency? If the larger number of older people are living longer but experience fewer years of ill health, the future need for long term care for each person may reduce and the total may not go up very much from what it is now. If people experience no longer periods of ill health than the current generation, the need for long-term care for each person will be the same, although the total need will rise. If, on the other hand, people experience more ill health for longer, the need for long-term care will increase both for each individual and in total.

The emerging evidence from the United States points in the direction of the first option – what we might call the Queen Mother Alternative – long and active life followed by a short illness. That seems intuitively right since we will be starting to see the first pensioners who have been supported by the NHS since birth. Geriatricians have argued that there are in practice very many ways to compress the period in which older people have severe dependency and to increase their years of independence.

However, there are other challenges which our ageing society will bring and these parallel the social and political changes already discussed. When Joan Collins was asked, after her recent fifth marriage, if she was worried about the age difference with her new partner Collins replied: 'If he dies, he dies.' Her confident assertion of her right to continue choosing her future stands for a generation now growing old disgracefully. All around us we can see the signs that the sweeping social change we associate with the baby boom generations of the 1950s and 1960s continues unabated. Not content with having created teenagers and defined youth rebellion they are now redefining middle age and beyond.

Still, why should this be a challenge? Surely a generation of assertive, independent older people is precisely what policies on pensions and health care were intended to achieve? The political problem is that the choices more and more older people are making, and the lives they are choosing to live, challenge fundamental pre-conceptions about how government, and society at large, views them. Yet whilst older people are changing, the public services they are offered remained rooted in the old paternalistic welfare culture. What does the state currently offer older people? Tea dances and day centres, an increasingly nugatory state pension and a health service where staff treat users as if they were children. The pensioners who went through the General Strike and endured the Depression are being joined by generations who never had it so good in the 1950s, have lived well since then and have no intention of being hard done by now.

As with many social changes, we can see this more clearly if we look at the United States. One of the most important pressure groups there is the American Association of Retired People (AARP). They are so powerful that reform of Social Security, the US state pension system, is described as a 'third-rail' issue: touch it and you die. It is said that in every US neighbourhood the shabby building in need of repair and decoration is the local school in stark contrast to the modern and well-maintained services for seniors. There already signs that change is on the way in the UK – think of the storm that engulfed the Labour government when it raised pensions by 75p a week, and the conspicuous lack of gratitude shown by pensioners when the Chancellor raised pensions by the single largest amount ever the subsequent year.

A political storm is gathering. An ageing population does not simply mean different demands on public services. It means a different public and a radically different electorate. Older people are growing in force There are simply more and more of them. Perhaps more importantly, they form an increasing proportion of the electorate. While turnout falls steeply amongst the under 35s it stays constant among the over 55s. Political parties have spent recent elections adopting increasingly absurd postures to woo the youth vote. The real contest is elsewhere. Whichever political party can fashion the right appeal to older voters across the board will be set fair for decades to come.

Older people have the power and a new welfare settlement seems inevitable. The continuing decline in the value of the Basic State Pension with the projection of an eventual fall to around 10 per cent of average earnings is not just morally indefensible but politically unsustainable. The increasing healthy life-span of older people also makes the state pension age of 65 an anachronism. Once a worker could expect a couple of years of life after retirement at 65, now ten or fifteen years is the norm. A change in the state pension age, perhaps raising it to 70, would allow a substantial increase in its level (to over £110 a week on current figures). Payment at such a level could trigger other changes. It would allow the ending of means testing for the Minimum Income Guarantee and the Pension Credit. This would free up resources for a greater increase in the state pension, perhaps to a level approaching a third of average earnings. Still not a king's ransom but adequate to live on and a good platform for any individual savings.

Such a settlement needs to be accompanied by a wider package of reforms. Here we return to the issue of long term care. The principled case for free personal care is overwhelming. It is a devastating cost which falls on a few individuals at random. It costs too much for each of us to insure against individually but it costs little when we insure ourselves collectively. This is precisely the same case that the Chancellor rightly makes for continuing to pay for the NHS through general taxation.

Electorally, the case for free personal care may also become overwhelming. Equally, an expectation of a longer working life would have to be matched by effective action against ageism in employment. This will be necessary anyway because changing demography changes the very basis on which we organise our labour markets. Professions ranging from accountancy through nursing to teaching are all built on the assumption that you can recruit new entrants at age 18 to 21 and keep them for the rest of their working lives. At the very least the shrinking number of young people will lead to increased competition for them and to higher wages for the educated and the lucky. At best, this should lead to a concerted attempt to transform how and who organisations recruit. A little noted impact of raising the state pension age to 65 for women between 2010 and 2020 is that the total UK workforce increases in size from 39 million in 2011 to 40.8 million by 2021. This will provide us with a mature, experienced cohort of workers. The question is, will we use them intelligently?

It remains to be seen whether the shift in the balance of the generations will lead to 'a new cleavage in politics'. However, the ageing population will accelerate demands for more personalised services than are currently available. A senior in one day centre was asked by a visitor whether she enjoyed the activities provided. The answer was blunt: 'No, but you have to do them to get the lunch'. The combination of political power with purchasing power will sweep such provision away.

The future(s)

There are many questions to which we don't yet know the answers. We are trying to generalise on the basis of emerging trends, but just as demography is not destiny nor is an individualist, atomised, consumerist society the ineluctable consequence of the social and economic changes we see around us. Thinkers in the 1950s and 1960s made many millennial predictions which have failed to materialise (hover-cars anyone?). Yet the lesson is not to stop predicting the future but to learn to predict possible futures and then ensure workers and organisations are sufficiently flexed to meet whichever challenges arise.

This process should lead to a cautious optimism about the future(s) of social care, its values and its skill base. We are seeing a diaspora of skills and values put into Sure Start, the Connexions service, community development within SRB areas and Primary Care Trusts. Even if it were possible for organisations to execute a successful 'land-grab', the changing nature of the workforce makes any contest about boundaries a zero-sum game, as workers become more individualistic in choosing which organisations to align themselves with.

Above all, the one thing that is needed for the future is the ability to nurture capacity: among individuals, families and communities. This is surely a core strength of social care at its best: recognizing the key roles that users and carers have to play in shaping and providing services, from the teenager in care assisting with the recruitment of the staff who will look after them to the 65 year old woman who is a major part of care-giving and support to her parents in their 90s. The future in all public services will be about empowerment, choice, individual tailored provision: a world to win.

3. The future aims and objectives of social care
Gerald Wistow

The purpose of the chapters presented in this book is to develop 'a coherent vision for social care in 2020.'[1] The task of preparing a set of aims and objectives to underpin such a vision might be addressed in two ways: the aims and objectives to be adopted in 2020; or those which are intended to be realised by 2020. The first approach would identify the aims and objectives to be developed for 2020 in the light of our current understandings and predictions about, for example, the needs, demands, expectations, values and governance arrangements which might be expected to apply some two decades hence. By contrast, the second approach takes 2020 as the end point rather than the beginning of the exercise. It attempts to project, from current experiences and aspirations, a coherent vision of the purposes and shape of social care to be achieved by 2020. By definition, therefore, it seeks to establish a desired destination for social care as a result of policy and implementation processes which are currently in place or which can and should be initiated in the intervening period. While partly being influenced by the need to prepare for tomorrow's problems today, they must also be capable of dealing with today's problems tomorrow.

These two approaches are not mutually exclusive. Each would produce scenarios which, ideally, should inform the other. They are, however, fundamentally different exercises, conducted for different purposes. The first is not only inherently more speculative and less certain than the second. It also implies a greater capability for what might be termed '2020 foresight' than experience suggests is realistic. The second approach is adopted here, therefore, not merely because it is, in principle, the more feasible but also for the pragmatic and utilitarian purpose of seeking to contribute to the debate about how social care might be shaped and fashioned over the next 17 or 18 years.[2] The challenge to be met, therefore, is to specify what kind of outcomes social care should be achieving as a matter of course by 2020. In turn, this requires us to identify the high level aims and objectives which would direct social care to those desired destinations. Thus the essential purpose of this chapter is to establish what values and objectives we would expect to be reflected routinely in the receipt (and, therefore, delivery) of such care in twenty years' time.

It may be argued that the same concerns for realism and utility would suggest that a twenty year time horizon is still excessively ambitious. Would it have been possible in 1980, for example, either to predict the shape of social care around the millennium or to plan for a set of outcomes to be realised by then? It was certainly not evident in 1980 that the period of virtually unchallenged state welfare was coming so rapidly to an end in social care so that, by the middle of that decade, local authority social service departments would be the minority provider of residential services (Wistow *et al* 1994). It is also doubtful if many observers would have predicted that, by the mid-1990s, social service departments would be so reliant on large numbers of front-line care staff in the independent sector, working with terms and conditions of employment (and not infrequently training) inferior to that of employees in the major supermarkets (Wistow and Hardy 1999). The real point of such examples, however, is not merely that they were unpredicted. They were also the unanticipated consequences of funding and workforce developments which were not planned in any meaningful sense. As a result, such examples can also be seen to reinforce the underlying purpose of this chapter and the approach it has adopted.

It is not enough simply to establish greater awareness of, and sensitivity to, emerging trends in the internal and external environments of social care. Trend planning, as Niskanen famously observed, is a predictive mechanism by which the present 'colonises the future' (Niskanen 1973). It predicts the future on the basis of assumptions rooted in the present or the past and which may be more or less comprehensive and more or less explicit. The case for the kind of exercise in which we are engaged here is for a form of analysis which not only anticipates but also shapes the future. Even if the consequences of a mixed economy of social care had been correctly predicted, it would still have been necessary to shape and re-shape those forces in accordance with explicit views about what constituted desirable (or even acceptable) outcomes, from the perspectives of service users, their families, their communities and front-line staff, and also within the context of the wider political economy.

Reference to social care outcomes inevitably introduces into the analysis questions about the values and principles of social care. If our purpose is as much to help shape as well as to anticipate the future, it necessarily raises questions – and choices – about what constitutes desirable directions and destinations. In other words, it requires at least a minimal framework of principles and purposes to guide the consistent development of policy and practice as well as to provide reference points for scrutiny, review and revision. The principle of empowerment through user involvement provides a useful example of why such frameworks and processes are necessary. While user engagement and empowerment have undoubtedly become more fully developed over the last twenty years in social care (especially compared with the NHS), there is also much evidence to demonstrate that it is not rooted in everyday routines and practices. If it had been treated in 1980 as a core element of an over-arching framework within which social care was being shaped, central and local government would have been routinely asking questions about the extent to which it had become embedded in mainstream systems and procedures. Was it part of the taken-for-granted assumptions about what constitutes everyday practice in social care? Alternatively, was it the province of special projects, 'add-ons' to the mainstream, whose horizons may become limited, in practice, to promoting user involvement as an end itself? Only by regular review and adjustment, within a guiding framework of values and principles, is such activity likely to become socially embedded within the culture of the sector as a whole.

Core values, principles and objectives in social care have undoubtedly become more fully developed since 1980 and their significance better understood in the process of building the current framework of services and care. Indeed, even those last two basic terms (services and care) have been seen to be conceptually problematic and unacceptable to the social movement which has grown up in the field of 'disability'. Yet, to some extent at least, such developments may be seen as the interpretation and re-interpretation of previous taken for granted assumptions. Moreover, they arise from the practical application by service users of values such as self realisation and self determination, especially in relation to matching individually defined needs with appropriate services. Almost by definition, such processes imply fundamental cultural change on the part of both providers and recipients of services. As such, they pose substantial challenges to the interests, values and beliefs of the respective parties and, as such, are unlikely to be resolved in the short term. Indeed, they demand systematically structured programmes of change management supported by training, confidence building and targeted funding, if they are to have any chance of becoming mainstream practice over any reasonable timespan. The alternative is to rely solely on individual champions and lengthy processes of osmosis, the results of which are entirely unpredictable in terms of time and geographical coverage.

The experience of introducing the principles of normalisation (Wolfensberger 1972) through the 'Ordinary Life' initiative is relevant here. It was initiated as long ago as 1981, but by the independent King's Fund rather than central or local government (King's Fund, 1980). In the first instance, its basic values and principles diverted sharply from everyday thinking and practice about services for the 'mentally handicapped'. Indeed, it was launched into an environment where it had been necessary for Peter Mittler to emphasise in the title of his recently published book that these individuals were 'People not Patients' (1979). The present author's experience of research during the first half of the 1980s illustrated the necessity to change basic attitudes. Semi-structured interviews with civil servants and NHS/local government managers produced unprompted challenges to the view that people with learning disabilities had a right to a 'life as close to the normal as possible':

> There are some people who think that the mentally handicapped should actually be asked what their views are.

> The mentally handicapped are no more sentient beings than that chair.

The apparently benign and worldly wise scepticism of the first comment was more commonly expressed than the extreme view of the second (but, in policy terms, very senior) respondent. Both, however, serve to separate, divide and marginalise groups with potential needs from the majority with less particular needs.

Such basic assumptions – or prejudices – are unlikely to be voiced in such circles today. Public attitudes have also changed substantially, partly as a result of less segregated services for learning. It would be wrong, nonetheless, to underestimate the extent of prejudice and discrimination that remains. The values and principles of the ordinary life initiative for people with learning disabilities have still to be universalised, even in Wales where there was a ten-year funded programme with, at least initially, strong political backing and a high profile (Felce *et al* 1998). The conceptual and implementation tasks inherent in designing new service models and training new categories of support worker against the grain of established thinking and routines have ensured that such developments have been slow and incomplete elsewhere in the United Kingdom (Department of Health 2001).

In services for people other than those with learning disabilities, change has been even more partial and fragmented. In the case of older people, for example, ageism and age discrimination continue to be enduring features of service cultures and public attitudes which, in turn, reinforce the over-modest expectations and aspirations of older people and their families (Help the Aged 2002). The title of the recent learning disability White Paper, 'Valuing People', is no less relevant to the service and wider social contexts older people and other groups experience (Department of Health 2001). Moreover, unlike the case of learning disabilities, the tension between 'medical' and other models of care remains to be resolved. The 'bed' continues to be the dominant unit of currency and the interface between hospital and social care systems continues to be professionally contested territory, as the case of intermediate care clearly highlights (Wistow *et al* 2002a).

These examples demonstrate that there is value in looking backwards in order to look forwards. The purpose of the current exercise is to lay the foundations for the development not only of a coherent vision for social care but also for the realisation of that vision within twenty years. The experience of the last two decades is relevant to that task precisely because it provides opportunities to learn about the need to combine clear objectives with the capacity and capability to deliver them. As long ago as 1988, David Towell was signposting literature about strategic management, organisational learning and leadership behaviour as necessary contributions to building 'an ordinary life in practice' (Towell 1988). Yet, it is questionable whether social care managers are even now equipped with sufficient background in the theory and practice of management and especially its application to their own particular contexts and environments. Similarly, it is indisputable that the shift to social care markets was initiated in a context where the underlying values of markets were antithetical to the basic values of social care (though a policy emphasis on choice and independence helped to bridge the gap). In addition, very few managers, at any level in the social care system, were equipped with an understanding of even the most basic concepts of economics, market development and market management (Wistow *et al* 1996).

Against that background, this chapter seeks to set out a clear sense of direction as a framework within which social care services will continue to improve and deliver better outcomes for individuals, their communities and wider society. In doing so, it is informed by two important and linked lessons from the last 20 years. First, that securing change in social care implies long term shifts in organisational, professional and social cultures; and, second, that delivering cultural change is one part of a wider implementation capability which needs to begin through a framework of values and principles that shape change to achieve desired outcomes.

Organising Social Care: History and origins

The statutory social services have existed in their current form only since 1971. Following the recommendations of the 1968 Seebohm Report (Report of the (Seebhom) Committee on Local Authority and Allied Personal Social Services, 1968) the previously fragmented children's and welfare services were unified under the responsibility of local authority social services departments (Hall 1976). They were established on a wave of optimism as the final foundation stone of a comprehensive and universalist welfare state, the 'fifth social service' (Townsend 1970) to follow the health, housing, education and social security services set up in the immediate post-war period. The origins of the Seebohm Report lay in concerns about the need to develop more preventative approaches to social work with young offenders, children and their families. When the report was commissioned, the focus was broadened to include welfare services as well, though its terms of reference were still expressed in terms of the need 'to secure an effective family service'. In practice, this circle was squared by defining family to include all kinds of households. Accordingly, the Report's central recommendation was for:

a new local authority department, providing a community based and family orientated service, which will be available to all. This new department will, we believe, reach far beyond the discovery and rescue of casualties, it will enable the greatest possible number of individuals to act reciprocally, giving and receiving service for the wellbeing of the whole community.

Later in the report, the aims of the new departments were further set out in the following terms:

We are convinced that if local authorities are to provide an effective family service they must assume wider responsibilities than they have at present for the prevention, treatment and relief of social problems...the resources at present allocated to these tools are quite inadequate... Moreover, the ways in which existing resources are organised and deployed are inefficient. Much more ought to be done in the fields of prevention, community involvement, the guidance of voluntary workers and in making fuller use of voluntary organisations.

In addition, the Report advocated that what it labelled social service (rather than services) departments should promote: service integration at the level of individuals, administrative unification, community involvement, community identity, citizen's participation, consumer choice and establishment of 'physical and social environments which people find it pleasant to live in'.

What is evident from these extracts – and may be a surprise for the modern first-time reader of Seebohm – is how contemporary its basic aims appear, and not least in its emphasis on the community dimension. For example, the Report calls for:

the personal social services to engage in the extremely difficult and complex task of encouraging and assisting the development of community identity and mutual aid, particularly in areas characterised by rapid population turnover, high delinquency, child deprivation and mental illness and other indices of social pathology. Social work with individuals alone is bound to be of limited effect in areas where the community environment itself is a major impediment of health to individual development.

In addition, it describes 'community identity' as being derived from 'common values, attitudes and ways of behaving which (community) members share and which form the rules which guide social behaviour within it'. In this respect, therefore, community development and participation are seen as vehicles for promoting 'the strong social control over behaviour which is characteristic of highly integrated and long-established communities'.

If the language and literary style now seem dated, many of these basic aims are at least partially echoed in the more recent policy lexicon of social exclusion and social inclusion, community capacity building and renewal, social cohesion, sustainable communities, customer responsiveness and democratic renewal. In addition, they bring us back to questions about the effectiveness of policy implementation. Does the apparent persistence of both problems and solutions in the field of social care suggest that the implementation of the Seebohm Report was a failure or, rather, that it failed to be implemented? In either case, what are the implications for pursuing objectives in the 21st century which are apparently similar to those endorsed in what Donnison called a 'great state paper' (Donnison 1968)? (Though, by contrast, Townsend was fiercely critical of its shortcomings (Townsend 1970).) This chapter is not the place to resolve such issues, however, their relevance here is to reinforce the suggestion, made above, that any discussion of aims and objectives for the next two decades should take into account the imperfect relationship between goal setting, on the one hand, and implementation capabilities on the other, as revealed in the history of personal social services since their inception.

Before beginning to identify more specifically a set of aims and objectives to provide direction to social care up to 2020, it is important to consider in a little more detail two of the principal forces which shaped the creation of social service departments and have remained significant influences on the aims and objectives of social care ever since. They can also confidently be expected to remain relevant over the next two decades. First, social care was born out of the final vestiges of the Poor Laws and, indeed, the new social services departments inherited some of the former's Victorian physical fabric. A more extensive inheritance, however, was the need finally to break through entrenched beliefs that such services and the people who received them were not part of mainstream society. The former 'welfare' services had existed on the fringes of the welfare state to tidy away the infirm, the mentally disturbed or mentally feeble, older people without the means for a dignified, self sufficient retirement and problem families on the boundaries of poverty, responsible parenting or criminal behavior. If the language of less eligibility was no longer heard, it lingered in at least some aspects of provision and, more generally, in wider social perceptions of social care services and their users. As a direct consequence, the Seebohm Committee argued for unified Departments on the grounds that it was 'justifiable to hope' that they would attract more resources.

The need for sustained investment is well demonstrated by the fact that it was not until the late 1960s that spending on what became the personal social services overtook the total for school meals, milk and welfare foods (Webb and Wistow 1982). Better funded, modern services were key, therefore, to universalising social care. Indeed, the Report was explicit that the new arrangements it was recommending should embody 'a wider conception of social services, directed to the wellbeing of the whole community and not only of social casualties'. Such a conception would, it hoped, spell 'the death knell of the Poor Law legacy and the socially divisive attitudes and practices which stemmed from it'. In similar vein, it argued for 'citizen's participation' in the 'planning, organisation and provision of social services'. This development was advocated on three grounds: local democracy, identification of need and 'above all' to reduce the 'rigid distinction between givers and takers of social services and the stigma which being a client has often involved in the past. The whole community 'consumes' the social services, whether directly or indirectly, as well as paying for them through taxation'.

In practice, social services departments have been recipients of sustained investment. Even during the Conservative Governments of 1979-97, they spent nationally (in all but one year) at least the additional two per cent per year, which was then generally agreed as necessary to maintain service levels in the face of rising demands. Such investments were secured even when local government expenditure as a whole was being reduced in the annual spending plans. If, however, social service departments have proved able to attract levels of resources consistent with Seebohm's aim of lifting them out of their poor law inheritance, it may be argued that it was at the expense of the Report's intention that their work should be directed at the 'wellbeing of the whole community and not only of social casualties'.

Throughout the Conservative years, the relative protection of social services departments' expenditure was secured partly on the grounds of its interface with the NHS (see below) but more particularly on the grounds that their services were directed at the 'most vulnerable' members of society' (Webb and Wistow 1982). In effect, therefore, the price of increased spending was targeting on those perceived as social casualties on the margins of mainstream society and, in turn, the neglect of the wider community wellbeing objective. Indeed, the broader community development role faded among the controversies of the Community Development Programme initiatives of the late 1970s' Callaghan Government. Despite Norman Fowler's subsequent enthusiasm for patch social work and his commissioning of the Barclay Report on community social work (Barclay 1982) the community dimension of the social services has never been developed nationally in the terms anticipated by Seebohm. In more contemporary terminology, they have tended to focus on social exclusion rather than social inclusion, thereby reinforcing perceptions that their client groups are the socially excluded rather than citizens of mainstream society with particular needs. As a result, and again in contemporary terms, it has been difficult to secure the 'middle class buy-in' necessary to establish and sustain social care as a universal service, notwithstanding the fact that many of the middle classes are actual or potential consumers of social care, indirectly if not directly. While their social control role (especially in respect of children, young people and their families) may also contribute to such perceptions, it is inescapably the fact that the adult groups they serve continue to experience prejudice, discrimination and other forms of exclusion. Such experiences are not only historically located in the Poor Law origins of social care in less eligibility rather than full citizenship. They are also reinforced by the failure to realise the community wellbeing role and to secure a recognition that the community as a whole are consumers of social care. All these continuing weaknesses must form the starting point for a re-emphasis on Seebohm's 'community diversion' as part of a vision for the future of social care.

The first public policy document to challenge such limitations was the White Paper *Modernising Social Services* (Department of Health 1998). Significantly, it started with the statement. 'social services are for all of us' and emphasised that 'all of us are likely at some point in our lives to need to turn to social services for support, whether on our own behalf or for a family member'. In addition, it argued that

> we all benefit if social services are providing good effective services for those who need them. Any decent society must make provision for those who need support and are unable to look after themselves. Breakdowns in services for young offenders, homeless people, or people with mental health problems can have damaging consequences for other people as well as individuals themselves.

Finally, it was explicit that social services 'do not just support a small number of social casualties, they are an important part of the fabric of a caring society. It is a concern for everyone that social services should be providing the best possible services'. This re-emphasis on universal, social care of the highest quality and of which we are all potentially consumers provides a basic starting point for our consideration of future aims and objectives. We return to this issue below but first we review one of the other fundamental factors responsible for the present shape and culture of social care: its relationship to the NHS and medicine.

Social Care and the NHS

It would be impossible to discuss the future aims and objectives of social care without reference to the NHS. The two services were placed under a statutory duty to collaborate with each other from 1974 and their respective shortcomings in fulfilling that duty have been the source of both criticisms and initiatives from central government ever since. One of the principal difficulties from the latter's perspective is that the division of responsibilities between the two services in 1974 left the centrally managed NHS dependent on locally governed personal social services to complete the implementation of fundamental NHS policies. Initially, this power-dependency relationship was most clearly apparent in relation to community care policies for reducing the role of long stay hospitals (Wistow 1987). Over time – and especially since the mid 1990s – it has been increasingly understood that access to acute care is similarly dependent on contributions by social services departments which delay or prevent admission to acute beds, facilitate earlier discharge and avoid re-admissions (Wistow 1995). This close but asymmetric relationship of dependence between the NHS and social care services (as well as other local authority responsibilities, especially housing) is a central feature of the terrain in which health service improvement policies are made and implemented. It is also increasingly recognised that the improvement of health and wellbeing depend even more on the contribution of local authorities and other partners. Yet, the current boundary between the NHS and local government rests on explicit decisions, taken in the 1970s that they should be administered separately.

The Seebohm Report specifically recommended that social care should have an administrative base in local government, independent of medicine. Its concern about the history of 'conflict and poor liaison' between the social work and medical professions was such that it recommended their organisations separation: 'in the case of medical officers of health, mutual misunderstanding with social workers has gone so far as to be a significant factor in an overall thinking on the future shape of social services'. As a result, home help services were removed from the medical officer of health (MOH) in 1971 and separate social services departments established alongside local government health departments led by the MOH. In 1974, however, the administrative separation of local government and the health service was completed when the boundaries of the two services were re-drawn on the basis of 'the skills of their providers' (Department of Health and Social Security 1970) rather than the needs of client groups. As a result, all medical and nursing staff transferred out of local government while hospital social workers transferred into it. An attempt to square the circle was made by drawing the geographical boundaries of local authorities responsible for social services to coincide with the new Area Health Authorities. The Secretary of State Sir Keith Joseph acknowledged that 'in a perfect world, the answer would be to unify health services within local government' (Thomas and Stoten 1974). In what was presumably his version of the 'real world' he was left to argue the benefits of geographical coterminosity through 'parallel reorganisations' However, his Labour shadow and predecessor (Richard Crossman) described it as 'a miserable middle way' which left services 'wobbling inbetween', neither taking over local authority community services by the NHS nor taking the NHS into local government (Crossman 1972).

Few public documents and statements since 1974 have failed to combine a recognition of the need for collaboration between the NHS and social services departments (and much less frequently, the wider local authority) with both praise for individual instances of progress and also the necessity for continuing improvement across the board. *Modernising Social Services* was typical in this respect:

> The National Health Service is a crucial partner in almost all social services work...if partner agencies are not working together, it is the user who suffers... Both health and social services authorities recognise this and many have worked hard...to enable users to receive the high quality, integrated services they need.... We know there is plenty of enthusiasm among staff and managers...to work together innovatively...and there have been many excellent examples of joint working... But we need to translate those individual examples of good practice into routine working at all levels and in all parts of the country. We are determined to overcome the obstacles to effective joint working that remain.

The governmental response to this analysis has been, and continues to be, an essentially managerialist mixture of exhortation, financial incentives and penalties, requirements for integrated planning, performance assessment and legislative change, the last being carried through under the terms of the 1999 Health Act. *The NHS Plan* (Department of Health 2000) and the most recent post-budget Command Paper *Delivering the NHS Plan* (Department of Health 2002) reflect a broadly similar approach but with one crucial addition: they advance the possibility of structural change through the delegation of specified local authority social care responsibilities to Care Trusts, that is NHS bodies seen as a new level of Primary Care Trust (PCT). Subsequent guidance raised the possibility that such Care Trusts might also encompass housing and the other local authority services (Bell

2001). This development is of fundamental significance both to the future of social care and also because it represents a complete reversal of government policy.

Labour's initial stance was to reject structural change and focus on providing through the 1999 Health Act an enabling framework for the partnership working which was seen to be one of the hallmarks of the third way in the NHS and local government. Thus, it rejected the Commons Health Committee recommendation in 1998 that a structurally integrated health and social care system was 'the only sensible long-term solution to end the current confusion' (House of Commons Health Committee 1998). Its grounds were that the Health Act's new (but permissive) operational flexibilities would provide 'a framework to develop working arrangements from the ground up' (Department of Health 1999).

Modernising Social Services had argued that 'major reorganisation of service boundaries – always a tempting solution – does not provide the answer. This would simply create new boundaries and lead to instability and diversion of management effort'. This tone had become very different by the publication of the NHS Plan, however. Not only did the latter introduce the possibility of structural integration through Care Trusts but, although 'normally' to be established by agreement, it also announced that the government would take powers to impose such arrangements where partnerships were ineffective or services were failing. Three months later, in his speech to the Annual Social Services Conference, the Secretary of State emphasised that compulsion would follow in such circumstances: 'there is a choice, partnership, including Care Trusts, can be established by you or they will be established by me.' *Delivering the NHS Plan* ends on a similar, threatening note. After announcing arrangements for charging social services if beds are blocked and the intention to introduce other incentives, including financial incentives for the voluntary take up of Care Trust status, it warned that 'if radical change is needed, we will introduce it'.

This background is paralleled in the family and child care sector by speculation that the Climbie enquiry will lead to be no less radical structural changes, together with the exploration by some local authorities of the possibility of combining family and children's services with education services. The starting point for considering the future aims and objectives of social care, therefore, is one of substantial structural instability. It cannot be automatically assumed that social care will be provided through the unified Seebohm Departments; nor that it will be provided through local government; nor that both the former children's and welfare functions will continue to be located within the same organisations. Given that the focus of this chapter is on adult services (in essence the former welfare functions), the possibility of structural change for children and family services is treated here as simply a contextual factor which might facilitate the promotion of radical options for adult services. In other words, future aims and objectives for social care will need to take into account the structural configuration of social care services both separately and as a whole, together with the nature of their relationship to the NHS and local government. Seebohm's basic structural building blocks of administrative unification within an organisation independent of medicine all need to be reviewed. It will be argued below, however, that such a review should be founded on an assessment of the enduring values and characteristics of social care and the outcomes it is designed (or re-designed) to realise.

Towards 2020

The previous analysis of the origins and history of the current organisational framework for social care is important for a number of reasons. First, it clarifies some of the most important aspects (structural, financial and cultural) of the inheritance within which any consideration of future aims and objectives will be located. Second, it highlights the importance of implementation capacity and capability as essential features of effective objectives setting. Third, it identifies the interdependence of values, principles and outcomes and their role as the driving force for developing aims and objectives for 2020. Fourth, it emphasises that structures and processes or systems are logically subordinate to values, principles and outcomes. As means rather than ends, they should flow from future aims and objectives and not be allowed to determine them. Against that background this chapter now seeks to address the following questions: What outcomes does social care seek to realise? What are the values, principles and characteristics of social care associated with those outcomes? What aims and objectives are implied by these outcomes? What organisational and other implementation frameworks are likely to facilitate the achievement of these outcomes?

Social care outcomes

The outcomes of social care tend to be most frequently associated with the wellbeing of individuals. In practice, however, its central purpose can be seen as that of maximising the wellbeing of individuals, their networks, communities and wider society. In other words, we may identify three linked but nevertheless distinct categories of social care outcomes: individuals, community and governance (see Box 1). This concern for both individual and wider outcomes stems from two principal sources: first, individual wellbeing is positively facilitated by the quality and quantity of personal relationships, together with other

---

Box 1 Social care desired outcomes

Individuals
- Autonomy (choice)
- Independent living
- Participation in valued lifestyles
- Interdependence
- Outcome-related processes

Community
- Communities that care
  Social, psychological and practical support
- Communities that accept
  Minimal prejudice, discrimination, exploitation
  Acceptable levels of risk
- Social inclusion and cohesion
- Sustained health and wellbeing

Governance
- Holistic perspective at all levels
- Impelementation/delivery capacity and capability
- Appropriate balance of social care and medicine
- Active citizens
- Vibrant local democracy (including scrutiny/accountability)
- Joined-up government – causes not symptoms
- Best value (cost and quality)

aspects of their socio-economic and physical environments. Second, the same influences can also depress levels of individual wellbeing. 'Good' social care outcomes at the individual level require, at the collective level, therefore, the existence of communities that care or otherwise facilitate individual wellbeing. We return to characteristics of such communities later but first examine in more detail the notion of individual wellbeing. As a desired outcome of social care for individuals, wellbeing has been associated with enabling them to maximise their abilities and opportunities for autonomous decision making, independent living and participation in liftstyles valued by wider society. The last of these three dimensions is arguably assuming greater importance in a society increasingly characterised by consumerism and by the expectation that wants and needs will be satisfied as immediately as possible in a 24/7 'now' culture. In this context, the language of enabling will need to be replaced more fully by that of empowerment.

Changes in lifestyles and household formation may be expected to make traditional forms of congregate living less attractive and place an even higher value on independent living as a desired outcome. However, conventional definitions of 'independent living' as 'maintaining people in their own home for as long as possible' will need reviewing to take into account opportunities for engagement with others and participation in valued lifestyles. Independence as enforced, rather than chosen, isolation is a poor outcome for any of the groups accessing social care and is not normally associated with wellbeing. It is, rather, individual capabilities for independent living accompanied by – and as a consequence of – involvement in family and wider community life that constitutes an indicator of high quality outcomes in social care.

Stroke care provides a useful example of how a restricted definition of independent living may lead to poor quality outcomes for individuals and/or their carers. From the professional perspective, successful outcomes may be associated with the recovery of relatively minimal levels of physical independence (for example, in dressing, eating, washing or walking). In such circumstances, people who have experienced a stroke may be said – especially from the perspective of the hospital – to have achieved a capacity for independent living.

There are at least three problems with this definition of independent living as a successful outcome of care. First, it does not take into account the existence of co-morbidities and perhaps most especially the incidence of depression, which one study found among 36 per cent of survivors living in the community five years after their stroke (Wilkinson *et al* 1997). Second, there is considerable evidence that carers of such individuals experience strain and ill-health themselves: a review of 20 studies found that between 34 per cent and 52 per cent of carers of stroke patients suffer from depression and three studies showed that the depression of patients was positively associated with depression in carers (Han and Haley 1998). Third, it neglects the contribution of successful inter-personal relationships and engagement in community living as critical dimensions of a valued lifestyle. In short, independence as a valued outcome may best be seen as independent living made possible through patterns of interdependence with families, friends and the wider community. It is, therefore, an individual outcome fully realised only in tandem with, and as an expression of, collective outcomes. More specifically, successful independent living depends on social inclusion both to make it happen and to ensure that it is sustainable. Independence and social inclusion are, therefore, themselves interdependent rather than being conceptually or empirically distinct.

If the concept of wellbeing is also considered as a collective outcome, at least two dimensions deserve attention: the community and governance dimension. First, autonomy, independent living and valued lifestyles each have implications for wider society. For example, autonomy and independent living are both potentially challenges to traditional conceptions of risk as held both by families and wider society. Such challenges will arguably be reinforced by continuing trends in social and, more especially, geographical mobility. It is possible, therefore, that the more autonomy and independent living are realised as outcomes for older people or those with mental, learning or physical disabilities, the more it will expose them to risks which their families, social networks and the wider community will find it difficult to accept. Greater public debate is likely to be necessary to establish what may be termed 'the social limits to risk' in this context. The exploration of such issues is an essential element in building the degree of public confidence and community acceptance necessary to underpin independent living.

Independent living as a desired and successful outcome also has collective implications in the sense that the ability of individuals to maintain and regain their independence appears to be related to the quality and quantity of their family and social networks as providers of emotional and practical support (Godfrey and Randall 2002). In other words it has implications for all of us in terms of our understandings, attitudes and behaviours. Again, therefore, it would be desirable to review established conceptualisations of this outcome and recognise the need to re-define it as independence through interdependence and social integration. Finally, in this context, the reference to attitudes and behaviours highlights the crucial importance to outcomes for individuals of outcomes at the wider community level in respect of reductions in prejudice, discrimination and exploitation.

The governance dimension of wellbeing as a collective outcome concerns the contribution of social care to the realisation of wider public policy objectives and outcomes. First, as individuals do not (generally) exist in isolation from their communities, so social care does not exist in isolation from other areas of public policy. Indeed better integrated/co-ordinated outcomes from different parts of government is a public policy outcome which has eluded governments of all hues, though in its advocacy of 'joined up' government, the present administration has given it the highest priority since JASP in the early 1970s (Central Policy Review Staff 1975).

In this respect, therefore, the most general governance outcomes to which social care might contribute would be provided by evidence of effective partnership working across a wide range of sectors, services and agencies to secure improved levels of health and wellbeing. It will imply a core social care contribution through Local Strategic Partnerships (under local government's new power to promote and improve economic, social and environmental wellbeing) to produce community strategies, which in turn secure sustainable communities (DETR 2000). More specifically, the outcomes of such contributions would include: the reduction of social exclusion; the increase in social inclusion and social cohesion; economic and social renewal in neighbourhoods with high levels of deprivation; reductions in inequalities; the renewal of local democracy and accountability and a more active civil society.

Such outcomes are notable in three respects: first, they are all associated with the health improvement (as opposed to health service delivery) agenda; second, they are contemporary expressions of

Seebohm's development agenda for the community as a whole; and third; they represent community characteristics fundamental to enabling the personal fulfillment and wellbeing of the individuals and groups for whom social care has special responsibilities. Thus they represent desired outcomes of social care both in terms of its general role in community capacity building and also the contribution of that capacity to the lifestyles of groups with particular needs and requirements.

The individual, family, social network and 'whole' community roles are, therefore, fully interdependent in terms of realising each of the three categories of outcomes in social care. Indeed, one of the strengths of social care is that, at its best, it has placed great emphasis on developing a holistic perspective on individuals in relation to their needs, services and communities. The three dimensions of this perspective have been defined elsewhere by the author and colleagues (Wistow *et al* 2002a):

- **the whole person** in terms of their needs and wishes together with the physical, social and psychological factors which shape their capacity for independent living, as they define that concept.

- **the whole system** of care services, in terms of both a comprehensive range of services and also an interdependent network of interventions which interact in ways which make such forms of independent living possible.

- **a whole community approach** which recognises that individuals rarely sustain valued, independent lifestyles in isolation from the social networks which not only promote physical and mental wellbeing but also – and in consequence – make independent living valued and sustainable. In other words, the focus on independence should recognise that, in most cases, independence is preserved, restored and sustained through patterns of interdependence.

Again, it follows that a key governance outcome for social care would be to demonstrate that each of these dimensions is realised in practice. It is in this respect that the nature of the relationship with the NHS is so important. The author and colleagues have argued elsewhere, with particular reference to intermediate care for older people, that there is a tension between the drivers of day-to-day NHS policy and practice, on the one hand, and the emerging evidence-based understandings of how individuals actually retain and re-gain their independence, on the other (Wistow *et al* 2002a). For example, a study of 100 patients who suffered a fractured neck of femur found that the patients thought their own motivation and help from family and friends was more important in their ability to regain health and confidence than professional help. The availability of informal support was found to be an important factor in determining whether particular individuals were able to return home rather than enter institutional care (Wistow *et al* 2002b).

The acute medical model has traditionally given insufficient weight to understandings such as these which support the importance of seeing the individual as a whole, developing their strengths and promoting their psycho-social adjustment, as well as optimising defined aspects of their physical functioning. In this context, the ability of social care to operate as part of a wider local authority with both a community leadership role and the ability to co-ordinate housing, leisure, life-long learning, transport and other services is of critical importance. A particular example of the difference between medically and socially successful outcomes is provided by the concept of a 'safe discharge'. Policy and practice guidance for the NHS and social care rests on the notion that the underlying requirement to be satisfied is that any discharge should be clinically safe: an individual should not be placed at risk through the absence of services which can only be provided in a hospital environment or which, in practice, are not available outside it. From a non-clinical perspective, however, the notion of a safe discharge extends to the community safety and crime reduction perspective: is there a safe home and community in which the individual can regain their confidence and physical independence, free from the fear or actuality of crime? Social Service Departments, as members of the wider Local Strategic Partnership and its associated Community Safety Partnership are well placed to develop and realise this wider perspective from their local authority base and its wider partnership with (Regional) Government Office Crime Reduction policies. Whether or not social care should continue to have a base independent of medicine, it would seem necessary for the achievement of both health and wellbeing outcomes that it should be in a position to provide an effective counter-weight to the dominant medical model.

A final aspect of social care outcomes to be noted here is that in personal care services the process is often an integral part of the outcome (Wistow and Hardy 1998). That is to say, the way in which services are delivered is, itself, an important outcome of service delivery. For example, users of home care services have been shown to place high value on characteristics of care such as kindness, caring attitudes, respect for dignity, reliability, unhurried care, consistency and continuity of care and carers (Henwood *et al* 1997). Inevitably, in services where the outcome is in any way related to the nature and appropriateness of the relationship between those who deliver and those who receive services, the process of delivery affects not only satisfaction with the service but also the response to, and impact of, service provision on wellbeing. For example, providers who have neither the skills, time nor attitudes necessary to build up confidence, motivation and capabilities on the part of users, those who can only provide *to* and *for* them, will succeed in making very little contribution to the latter's empowerment.

This section of the chapter has sought to identify a range of individual and wider outcomes of social care. Many of them are not new, though the chapter indicates areas in which they may require greater emphasis or adjustment in the light of contemporary expectations and trends. The fact that the articulation of many current desired outcomes is of long-standing is both a strength and a weakness. It is a strength because they tend to reflect long-held values and assumptions about what the social services and social care ought to achieve with, and on behalf of, individuals and their communities. It is a weakness because many of them have yet to be achieved in routine practice. The present government is focussing considerably more attention on social exclusion, social cohesion and democratic renewal as well as on the rights of individuals with disabilities and on individually centred care. 'Shifting the balance of power' is no less applicable, as a policy goal to social care than the NHS (and in some respects is further advanced in practice). Social care now has an important opportunity to work with the grain of public policy. The most important outcome of all in the next ten to twenty years could be to build on that opportunity so that the gap between intention and reality is less narrow than at any time in the history of social care.

From outcomes to aims and objectives

In terms of policy development, it is conventional to think in linear terms so that aims and objectives are successively defined and then implemented to achieve pre-determined outcomes. In practice, policy making and implementation is a much more 'messy' and non-linear process, in which both goal setting and implementation processes are mutually dependent and redefined in response to the unpredictability of experience and reality. We have deliberately begun with the logical 'end' of the policy process. Identifying the desired outcomes of social care places a necessary logic and order around the specification of aims and objectives to be achieved by 2020. It ensures that, in considering the future of social care, there is a framework and discipline for thinking back from desired (and, as far as possible, evidence-based) outcomes to an articulation of the aims and objectives which would be needed to delivery them. As Box 2 demonstrates, the outcomes previously identified can readily be translated into aims. These aims can in turn be translated into broad objectives, as Boxes 3, 4, and 5 illustrate, in relation to two of the initial aims.

Box 2 Aims of social care

- Sustained health and wellbeing
- Appropriate balance of social and health care
- Convenient and fair access to full range of service options
- Choice, independence and inclusion
- Communities that care and accept
- Effective implementation and delivery mechanisms
- Effective partnerships for community governance
- Demonstrable best value (cost and quality)
- Effective public scrutiny and accountability

Most of these aims and objectives have already been referred to above. Perhaps the most substantial one that have not been covered are choice and developing the provider mix. These two elements have been combined in social care through the development of managed markets within a mixed economy of care. There are, however, fundamental difficulties about both the concept of choice and also the operation of markets in social care, at least as they have developed since 1983. The concept of choice in social care is problematic for at least four reasons. First, some users of social care services do not voluntarily choose to access them. Rather, they are required to become service users as a result of legal or quasi legal procedures and proceedings. Second, the conditions which give rise to individuals and families needing to

---

Box 3 Convenient and fair access

- Full and timely information in appropriate formats and locations
- Open access at convenient times (24 x 7 x 52?)
- Transparent eligibility criteria
- Legal and civil rights
- Public support and acceptance
- Whole systems cultural change

Box 4 Full range of service options

- Holistic multi-disciplinary assessment
- Whole system of comprehensive and continuous care
- Plan for surplus capacity
- Stimulate provider mix
- Develop, pilot and mainstream new options (provider and provision)

Box 5 Appropriate social care and NHS balance

- Person-centred perspective and involvement
- Social care as diversion and bridge
- Prevention, retention, recovery of independence
- Community dimension
- Evidence based care pathways
- Holistic perspective

---

access services may militate against the exercise of choice (for example, frailty, confusion, mental health problems, times of personal and family crises, or the breakdown of caring relationship). Third, decisions about access to social care are, in most cases, relatively rare lifetime events. Unlike the purchase or choice of most consumer goods, we have little previous experience to guide or inform this set of choices. Yet they may shape our opportunities and lifestyles long into the future, notwithstanding the circumstances in which they may be taken but also the lack of knowledge on which we have to draw. Finally, the concept of choice is inherently flawed if there are too few options from which to choose, because of an absolute scarcity supply and/or a relatively narrow range of types of services from which to choose.

The need to promote greater diversity of provision and providers was one of the principal reasons for introducing social care markets advanced by the former Conservative government. In practice, however, the major driving force for their introduction was the need to cap social security spending. Local authorities were, therefore, expected by Ministers to use their purchasing power to drive down costs (Wistow *et al* 1996). Government and independent bodies repeatedly emphasised the opportunities for cost savings by contracting out supply to the independent sectors (see for example, Audit Commission 1996). As a result, large elements of personal care are apparently being provided by a poorly trained and ill paid workforce whose terms and conditions of employment may militate against providing good quality care (Wistow and Hardy 1998; King's Fund 2001; O'Kell 2002). In addition, the supply side in the residential and nursing home sectors is said to be in crisis with increasing numbers of homes leaving the market (Laing 2002; O'Kell 2002; Williams *et al* 2002). None of this is to suggest that social care markets are inherently unsustainable but they may have delivered cost savings at the expense of a workforce whose quality of employment experience is a significant determinant of the quality of care experienced by users. In addition, the dominant private sector has not obviously delivered high levels of innovation in the range of services, especially accommodation services. Ironically, current initiatives to sustain the care homes market may lend to the ossification of the supply side and delay the introduction of housing based alternatives through partnership between local government and housing associations.

Conclusions

Three major conclusions may be drawn from the above discussion. First, the desired outcomes identified for achievement by 2020 effectively constitute the aims which social care should adopt now in order to ensure that it is able to make appropriate contributions to the health and wellbeing of individuals and communities over the next two decades. Second, the enduring nature of some of these desired outcomes is not matched by evidence that they are routinely realised: quite the reverse in fact. This conclusion highlights the need to review the implementation capacity and capability of social care services. This concern is reflected in the current Government's target to secure more effective delivery in public policy and public services. It requires social care specific, as well as more general, solutions based on explicit implementation models which are widely understood within social care and are sensitive to the contexts, values and aims of this policy field.

The third issue for consideration relates to the structural context for social care and especially its relationship to health services. For the reasons discussed above, adult social care has a distinctive contribution to make to the development and delivery of holistic care within a community focused and whole systems perspective. There are legitimate grounds for concern about whether this influence – which needs in practice to be strengthened – would in fact be diluted if social care were to be absorbed within the NHS. Equally, the links to other local authority functions, which are critical to the holistic approach and also fundamental to wider policies to reduce social exclusion, would be weakened by the transfer of social care to the NHS. In addition, such an approach would be contrary to wider governance policies for the renewal of local democracy, especially given the scale and public sensitivity of social services departments' responsibilities.

Perhaps most fundamentally, however, structural integration is simply an ineffective means of achieving the outcome of integrated or seamless care at the level of individuals and their carers. The experience of Northern Ireland provides ample evidence of this case. Recent evidence demonstrates that integrated working at the front line suffers similar weaknesses to those encountered elsewhere in the UK (McCoy 2000). In addition, evidence collected in Northern Ireland as long ago as 1978 showed that the more fundamental difficulties were not those of structure but those associated with professional values, socialisation experiences and boundary maintenance (Report of the Royal Commission on the National Health Service 1978). The search for the 'right' structure is a persistent weakness in policy making for health and social care. The route to better outcomes for individuals with health and social care needs is through integrated care pathways organised around evidence-based protocols which specify the roles, responsibilities and sequence of interventions by the different professionals involved. Moreover, structural reform is a diversion from the real need for effective service integration in the short to medium term and, by itself, is unlikely to be effective in the long term. Shifting the administrative furniture de-stabilises organisations and detracts from their ability for day to day delivery.

The real case for structural reform rests on wider governance policies rather than ones for social care and focuses on the centrality of health improvement goals and the reduction of health inequalities to community strategies for sustainable communities. It also revolves around the case for strengthening local democracy, especially in a context where the services of greatest significance to local people are subject to little local democratic influence or accountability. Each of these governance arguments points in the direction of bringing the NHS (or the commissioning functions) into regional and local government. It is a major weakness in the proposals for regional government that only the public health responsibilities of the NHS will become within the remit of the Regional Assemblies (and then only in an advisory capacity). The introduction of unitary local authorities as a concomitant of regional government provides a unique opportunity to pilot the integration of local government and the NHS through actual or virtual organisations. PCTs which are coterminous with unitary authorities could be brought into the local democratic system or joint appointments at directorate levels could achieve high levels of organisational integration and accountability. Crossman's 'miserable' middle way could be removed and Joseph's 'ideal world' created – at least in experimental form – in all or parts of the first regions which vote for Regional Assemblies. Democratising the NHS would, therefore, be part of a wider process of giving power to local people and exposing the NHS to the local forces of public accountability which would so greatly improve its effectiveness. Whether this aim is part of our 2020 vision depends on the confidence and imagination of those responsible for social care and local Government more generally.

Endnotes

1   In commissioning this contribution, IPPR agreed that it should focus on social care for adults and not encompass services for families and children.

2   A declaration of personal interest should be made as it may have affected the choice of approach and definition of objectives and desired outcomes: by 2020, the author's mother would be 100 and he would be 74.

Bibliography

Audit Commission (1996) *Balancing the Care Equation* Community Care Bulletin No 3 London: HMSO

Barclay P (1982) *Social Workers: their role and tasks* Report of a Working Party, London: Bedford Square Press

Bell C (2001) *Care Trusts – The Application and Consultation Process and the Governance Arrangements* London: Department of Health

Central Policy Review Staff (1975) *A Joint Framework for Social Policy* London: HMSO

Crossman RHS (1972) *A Politician's View of Health Service Planning* Glasgow: University of Glasgow

Department of the Environment, Transport and the Regions (2000) *Preparing Community Strategies: Government Guidance to Local Authorities* London: DETR

Department of Health (2002) *Delivering the NHS Plan* Cm 5503, London: The Stationery Office

Department of Health (2001) *Valuing People: A New Strategy for Learning Disability for the 21st Century* London: The Stationery Office

Department of Health (2000) *The NHS Plan* Cm 4818 London: The Stationery Office

Department of Health (1999) *Government Response to the First Report of the Health Committee on the Relationship between Health and Social Services* London: The Stationery Office

Department of Health (1998) *Modernising Social Services* Cm 4169 London: The Stationery Office

Department of Health and Social Security (1970) *National Health Service: The Future Structure of the NHS* London: HSMO

Donnison D (1968) 'Seebohm – the Report and its Implications' *Social Work* 25.4

Felce D, Grant G, Todd S, Ramcharan P, Beyer S, McGrath M, Perry J, Shearn J, Kilsby M and Lowe K (1998) *Towards a Full Life* London: Heinemann Butterworth

Godfrey M and Randall T (2002) *Communities that Care: Developing a Framework of Risk Assessment and Prevention Approaches Relevant to Older People* Leeds: Nuffield Institute for Health

Hall P (1976) *Reforming the Welfare* London: Heinemann

Han B and Haley W E (1998) 'Family Care giving for Patients with Stroke: Review and Analysis' *Stroke* 30.7 quoted in Robinson M (2002) *Moving on After a Stroke: A Structured Literature Review* Leeds: Nuffield Institute for Health

Help the Aged (2002) *Age Discrimination in Public Policy: A Review of Evidence* London: Help the Aged

Henwood M, Lewis H and Waddington E (1997) *Listening to Users of Domiciliary Care Services: Developing and Monitoring Quality Standards* Carshalton Beeches and Leeds: United Kingdom Home Care Association and Nuffield Institute for Health

House of Commons Health Committee (1998) *The Relationship between Health and Social Service* Vol I, London: The Stationery Office

King's Fund (1980) *An Ordinary Life* Project Paper No 24, London: King's Fund Centre

King's Fund (2001) *Future Imperfect? Report of the King's Fund Care and Support Inquiry* London: King's Fund

Laing W (2002) *Calculating a Fair Price for Care* Bristol: Policy Press

Mittler P (1979) *People not Patients* London: Methuen

McCoy K (2000) *Review of Care in the Community* Social Services Inspectorate, Department of Health, Social Services and Public Safety, Northern Ireland

Niskanen WA (1973) *Bureaucracy, Servant or Master? Lessons from America* London: Institute of Economic Affairs

O'Kell S (2002) *The Independent Care Homes Sector: Implications of Care Staff Shortages for Care Delivery* York: Joseph Rowntree Foundation

Report of the Royal Commission on the National Health Service (1978) Research Paper No 1, London: HMSO

Report of the (Seebohm) Committee on Local Authority and Allied Personal Social Services (1968) Cmnd 3703, London: HSMO

Thomas N and Stoten B (1974) 'The NHS and Local Government: Co-operation or Conflict?' in Jones K (edit) *The Yearbook of Social Policy in Britain 1973* London: Routledge and Kegan Paul

Towell D (1988) 'Managing Strategic Change' in Towell D (edit) *An Ordinary Life in Practice* London: King's Fund

Townsend P (1970) *The Fifth Social Service* London: Fabian Society

Webb A and Wistow G (1982) 'The Personal Social Services: expediency, incrementalism or systematic social planning?' in Walker A (edit) *Public Expenditure and Social Policy* London: Heineman

Wilkinson P R, Wolfe C D, Warburton F G, Rudd A G, Howard R S, Ross-Russell R W and Beech R R (1997) 'A Long Term Follow Up of Stroke Patients' *Stroke* 28.3 1997 quoted in Robinson M (2002) *Moving on After a Stroke: A Structured Literature Review* Leeds: Nuffield Institute for Health

Williams J, Netten A, Hardy B, Matosevic T and Ware P (2002) *Care Home Closures: the Provider Perspective* Discussion Paper 1753/2, Canterbury, London and Manchester: Personal Social Services Research Unit

Wistow G, Waddington E, Fong Chiu L (2002a) *Intermediate Care: Balancing the System* Leeds: Nuffield Institute for Health

Wistow G, Herbert G, Townsend J, Ryan J, Wright D, Ferguson B (2002b) *Rehabilitation Pathways for Older People after Fractured Neck of Femur: Executive Summary* Leeds: Nuffield Institute for Health

Wistow G and Hardy B (1999) 'Domiciliary Care: Mission Accomplished? *Policy and Politics* 27.2

Wistow G, Knapp M, Ford J, Kendall J, Manning R (1996) *Social Care Markets: Progress and Prospects* Buckingham: Open University Press

Wistow G (1995) 'Aspirations and Realities: Community Care at the Crossroads' *Health and Social Care in the Community* 3.4

Wistow G, Knapp M, Hardy B and Allen C (1994) *Social Care in a Mixed Economy* Buckingham: Open University Press

Wistow G (1987) 'Joint Finance: Promoting a New Balance of Care in England?' *Intermediate Journal of Social Psychiatry* 33.2

Wolfensberger W (1972) *The Principles of Normalisation in Human Services* Toronto: National Institute on Mental Retardation

4. The workforce for social work and social care

Liam Hughes

This paper is an exercise in 'blue sky' thinking about the future workforce and the nature of education and training for social work and social care. In the light of the trends and possibilities sketched out in the previous two chapters, what are the implications for staffing in 2020? Although this period of time may seem a long one, it represents only half the working life of a young professional entering social care and social work this year.

'Leaning into the future' is a difficult and uncertain art. Some of the predictions in this chapter may prove correct and others will be wide of the mark. History teaches us that we usually misjudge the most important trends and underestimate their impact. The real reason to think long term is to give us a wider context for the decisions we face today, and to strengthen our orientation towards new experiences. This is a good time to develop a longer term perspective: in social work and social care we are currently in an in-between state, one of leaving the old but not yet having arrived in the new. It is a period of both anxiety and potential and therefore exactly the time to look ahead.

As has been said many times before, in seeking to understand the future we need to look to the past. There have been some recurrent themes about the nature of social work and social care, revisited in each generation. Firstly, what are they, and what is it that distinguishes them uniquely as fields of practice? Are they professions or occupations? Are they generic or specialist? Secondly, how do they relate to neighbouring fields of practice such as teaching, nursing and medicine, youth and community work and early years work? Thirdly, as other services are reconfigured and new services introduced, will professional boundaries be realigned to follow them?

In the sections that follow, I will examine some of the implications for training and education of current public policy, looking first at social work and social care, and then at the Government's new initiatives to deal with social exclusion. I am taken by Bill and Charlie Jordan's description (2000) of social work as 'the dog that didn't bark'. Given the vast experience of social workers in poor neighbourhoods, and the aspirations of the Seebohm Report for comprehensive community services, why hasn't social work as a profession been more central to the fight to overcome social exclusion and to regenerating local communities? Some Social Service Departments have been actively involved in developing local initiatives but the impression is that social work has been seen by government as part of the problem rather than part of the solution. Over a long period, the official definition of social work has become narrower, and community and groupwork approaches have been placed elsewhere.

This leads me to a brief examination of the history of social work and its related disciplines. The chapter looks firstly at the early part of the twentieth century when social work was being established, and then at the long-running debate about the nature of the professions. It then considers in more depth the postwar period in the UK and at some of the new policy initiatives introduced since 1997.

The longer-term implications are examined in relation to some specific examples from the vantage point of 2020: Early Years Services, Sure Start, the Youth Justice Service and Connexions. These fields of activity have a strong affinity with social work and social care. They are personal services which involve counselling, group activity and community engagement. They are typical of the new configurations which have been designed around the needs of service users in relation to social inclusion. These new agencies share one common feature which is that they are highly focused on delivering specific objectives. Whilst they take staff from a variety of backgrounds, they are training them together to meet these objectives. In each case there has been curriculum development based on specific core competences.

This raises questions that may be uncomfortable for generic social work and social care about the nature and comparative effectiveness of the new specialist services, the roles of the agencies that provide them, and the needs that are being met. It also reopens a debate that has been going on for over a century about the scope of social work, its focus on casework and its wider role in community development and the prevention of social distress. Social care is already highly specialised in its nature, and the unity of social work within Social Service Departments is being tested by the internal separation into specialisms.

This opens up the prospect of service integration with other agencies and the unification of professional training across related disciplines, and the chapter explores this possibility through the example of Learning Difficulty.

My starting point, for the sake of promoting argument and debate, is that our public services have often failed because they have been built around the needs of agencies and professions, rather than service users. They would do well to reflect on the changes taking place in the better performing public service and commercial organisations to put customers at the centre of the picture and design services around them. An important aspect of the modernisation of public services has been the search for more responsive approaches that can avoid the rigidity of traditional welfare bureaucracies. These have often become tied down by procedures and the burden of rationing and have sometimes lost their focus on outcomes.

Social work and social care, for all their success in advocacy and individualised solutions have also experienced these problems and suffered from excessive bureaucracy. This is ironic, given the origins of the unified Social Service Departments (SSDs). They were a necessary invention in the 1960s because Education and Health had not given sufficient attention to personal support for vulnerable and socially excluded pupils and patients. At the time, only a strong corporate department could ensure that childcare, mental health and social welfare would flourish in the face of the limitations of the current medical model, the destructive history of institutionalisation and the neglect of child development.

Unified SSDs were established as a creative response to remedy this situation and to counter-balance the other 'big battalions' being introduced. They have been responsible for major improvements and innovations in social work and social care which should be remembered: removing children from long-stay hospitals, setting up community care for people with learning disabilities and mental health problems, providing support for older people in their own homes and in good quality residential settings, and improving fostering, adoption and residential care for children. They have also done well to keep children safe, although there have been inexcusable failures, and they have developed services to support families and involve them in case planning. SSDs have faced other demanding issues, especially the problem of the coordination of inter-agency working and that of rationing scarce resources. These have come to overshadow the positive developments in practice that have been promoted by SSDs.

Despite all the achievements, the public perception (or the media perception) is often one of poor practice and poor coordination. Service users and carers tend to be more positive, but this has yet to influence the general view. However, users and carers frequently criticise the complexity of the systems of care and provision. They are not interested in complex explanations about why services are fragmented or why there is conflict about who does what and who pays, least of all assertions that other agencies are no better.

During the 1990s concerted efforts were made to promote closer working between agencies and professions. These were for the most part successful, as far as they could go. However, inter-agency collaboration is difficult and time-consuming with high transaction costs. One 'solution' would be to redesign our public services so they meet the needs of service users in a more focused and acceptable way. Organisational forms should follow service functions and the related work processes. This might in turn involve the realignment of professional boundaries, the establishment of new career paths and the creation of new professions.

This is precisely what is happening in many of the new agencies. They have started by identifying needs, setting objectives based on these needs, designing the necessary processes and then establishing the organisational form. This has led them to address issues of workforce planning, establish core competencies and design service curriculums. As these organisations become stronger, and their identities more stable, they will define more and more the space that is left for the more traditional statutory occupations. This raises a number of problems and possibilities for social work and social care which are further explored below.

Some positive developments

Since 1997 there have been some important developments in education, training and professional standing for social work and social care. Firstly, the creation of the Training Organisation for Personal Social Services England will consolidate the national occupational standards for social care and social work, which themselves are built on detailed occupational and functional mapping. They will also confirm the central place of competence-based practice and learning in social work and social care. Secondly, the establishment of the General Social Care Council will serve to reinforce the boundaries of social work and social care as professions based on these competencies. Thirdly, the NVQ framework for social care already provides a good foundation for practice and lifts up traditionally neglected areas such as home care and residential care, so that practitioners can demonstrate their skills, knowledge and values. As the labour market tightens, and levels of training are enhanced, social care could become more socially and economically valued, although there will continue to be fierce competition to attract staff. Fourthly, the replacement of the current two year diploma in social work with a three year degree level qualification will strengthen it in comparison with other professions such as teaching, nursing and the allied health professions. These are positive developments for social work and social care.

So, too, are the major policy initiatives being promoted by the government to reduce social exclusion and promote regeneration, and to modernise other public services, notably health and education. To the extent that they are successful, they will provide a new and more sustainable context for social work and social care. The drive to end child poverty and renew local communities has led to an explosion of new initiatives including new Early Years services, Sure Start, the Children's Fund and the Connexions Service, the Action Zones for Education, Sport and Health, and Neighbourhood Renewal. It has also led to Welfare to Work programmes, Drug Action Teams and Youth Offending Teams. Local Strategic Partnerships have been established to link together district strategies for the economy, the environment, education, health and crime. New prototypes for better integrated services have been developed across health, social care, the voluntary sector and the private sector. These have all promoted creativity and innovation, in the attempt to move 'upstream' from major social problems. Whilst there are some difficulties with managing the complex environment created by these initiatives, they do represent a serious commitment by the Government to tackle some of the root causes of poverty and disadvantage.

The paradox is that in many of these programmes, the 'new kids on the block' are settling into specific niches in the new ecology of personal, family and community support that were once associated with social work. Indeed, lack of attention to them over recent decades has arguably produced the circumstances that have in turn forced social work into a more reactive mode. As a result, its scope has been narrowed to casework, with an emphasis on assessment and care management rather than direct therapeutic interventions. The groupwork and community development dimensions of social work that were part of the Seebohm vision have become increasingly invisible inside Social Service Departments.

Meanwhile, social care has developed rapidly, despite its fragmentation and low starting point, and there is now a complex relationship with its neighbours in health, early years and community services. To a considerable degree the philosophy of social care, and especially its use of social models of disability and its advocacy for human rights, have been imported into these areas. Many of the core skills and values demonstrated by social workers and social care practitioners are now in demand in the new services, which can often provide better working conditions and opportunities for practice than hard pressed SSDs. In order to maintain core services, SSDs will need to be made more attractive, particularly in relation to child protection, where the risks of staff shortage and limitations of skill and experience are most acute.

People doing this kind of work ten years ago might well have seen themselves as social workers and sought social work training; many today do not see themselves in any way as social workers. It is an identity they would not choose, and they prefer to be described by the name of the service and the people involved with it.

Despite this change in perception, it has been suggested that new Labour's policy agenda creates opportunities for the redemption of social work. Whilst the Government's programme for social reconstruction is ambitious and demanding, it requires compassion, skilful negotiations and dialogue with individuals, families and local organisations – exactly the mixture of competences represented by social work at its best:

> On the face of it, a programme for cultural and individual change, which emphasises sharing and mutuality and takes its exemplars and principles from the family, the

neighbourhood and the community, should provide fertile ground for a healthy, expanding social work profession (Jordan and Jordan 2000).

The implication is that whilst the scope of SSDs may be constrained by their statutory duties, the scope for social work and social care on a wider definition will expand. The question is whether they will be able to position themselves as core professions to take a full part in the government's programme, and whether it matters what they are called.

The history of social work (part 1)

The narrative that is often passed on to students portrays the history of social work as the inevitable journey towards a unified profession with a common foundation of generic education and training. There is a different historical account available, more uncertain and unstable, which draws attention to the changing variety of components associated with social work, their shifting boundaries and changing ideologies, and the subcurrents, twists and turns in their development. The significance of all this is that there was nothing inevitable in the creation of social work as a discrete profession, just as there is nothing inevitable about its survival.

The term 'social work' has been used most often to indicate social casework with individuals and families, although it has had a wider range of historical meanings. When it emerged in the late 19th century, it was associated with three streams of activity: family casework and individual support; settlement and community work, and occupational welfare (which was soon absorbed into personnel work). Group care settings were seen as being outside social work at that time and were associated, for example, with the workhouse, hospital, orphanage and industrial school. Recent research has outlined how settlement work grew out of dissatisfaction with the limitations of casework, and how it contained the seeds of adult education, youthwork and community development (Gilchrist and Jeffs 2001). The debates from this period – about strengthening communities, reinforcing education and training, preventing crime and providing useful leisure – have a remarkably contemporary ring to them.

Social casework also developed during this period, with the joint lectures committee setting up training in almsgiving and charity, the law, family and character, children and the personal qualities of the workers. The debate that followed in the early years of the 20th century on the reform of the Poor Law raised difficult questions about the proper extent of universal provision and more local responses to distress, about the nature of personal support through social work and social welfare and about individual moral obligation and community responsibility. Again, with the recent trend towards 'remoralising' public policy, there is a modern resonance in the turn of the century struggles to 'place' social work and differentiate it from other activities, such as the relief of poverty or medical services.

Two subsequent historical moments in the US are of particular note. The publication of Mary Richmond's *Social Diagnosis* (1917) gave social work a theoretical framework and some psychological tools of practice. It was to be holistic, taking account of the inner world of the individual, the family circumstances and the condition of the local community. It was to be systematic, based on observation and knowledge, and it was to have defined processes and move through some well-defined steps.

Social work now had a methodology on which to build a unified profession. In the following decades there was considerable debate about the extent of the boundaries of the profession, and the relationship between the social work functions and the agencies employing them. For example, in 1929 the Milford Conference in the US debated the commonality of casework as a method wherever it was to be practiced (AASW 1929). There was a strong impulse by some employers at that time to mirror the emerging nursing boundaries of medical, children and psychiatric practice and to create distinct and separate streams of social work training for each. However, the urge to create a strong united voice for social work in the face of medicine and education moved delegates in the opposite direction, towards generic, university-based education backed up with specialised practice placements. The less well known elements of the debate concerned the balance of academic to practical training, and the conditions for learning in 'the practicum'. There was some concern that the field was not prepared to carry the weight of practice support without the creation of education units.

If Richmond's work laid the foundation for the development of social work as a profession that could be practiced in any agency, then the Milford Conference established that there would be a unified approach to social work education and training, and the creation of a graduate profession in the US. In due course the UK followed the unified approach to training and education, but was slow to accept the need for graduate standing for the profession. As a result, it lagged behind teaching and nursing. This raises questions about the nature of professions and their legitimacy.

Some thoughts about professions

There are, very broadly, three main approaches to understanding professions. Freidson (1970) argued that professions seek to organise control over their working patterns, their knowledge and their education. Only the professional group can understand the specialist and make judgements about the appropriateness of a practitioner's work or the validity of professional education based on expertise. This first view of professions, the 'occupational control' view, is about power and occupational closure. Payne (1996) points out that social work education had been in the hands of professionals and that supervision had been provided by practitioners. These are significant signs of a profession. However, departmental management had been increasingly general and diverse, and social work had proved incapable of defending itself from adverse social reaction and political pressures unlike medicine and the law. (Since then, of course, both these professions have faced public attack.)

Wilensky (1963) proposed that all occupational groups were professionalising: developing unique bodies of knowledge and skill that marked them out from other occupations. As the discussion of labour intensified in complex modern societies, so occupations arose and moved towards professional status. Etzioni describes teaching, social work and nursing as semi-professions, each managing its separation from other occupations, but without the autonomy given by society to medicine, the law and the church (1969). This second view of professions, the 'process view', highlights issues about the stage of separation of social work on its journey from occupation to profession and invites us to make comparisons with other fields such as nursing and teaching. The uncertain association of professional status with higher education has been problematic for social work in the UK, given the earlier movement in teaching and nursing to graduate status, and social work's late arrival as a graduate profession. However, the traditional professions have themselves experienced a sea-change as they have come under much closer scrutiny, and lost ground.

A third way of understanding professions examines the traits of an occupation, including a wide knowledge base, particular skills and practices, systematic theory, levels of authority and sanctions, ethical codes and the social mandate for practice. Occupations are tested against these traits, to identify limitations and gaps, and place them on a professional hierarchy.

Historically, social work has not exercised direct disciplinary powers over its professionals, its social mandate has been uncertain, its knowledge base has been eclectic, and its theoretical foundations have been contested. Munro (1998) describes the poor track record of evaluation in social work, and the need for reflective practice to be linked to empirical research. She argues that despite these limitations there is an evidence base for the effectiveness of social work. For example, McDonald and Sheldon (1992) identify nearly one hundred evaluative studies with acceptable methodologies, of which 75 percent show positive results. These were interventions using cognitive and behavioural approaches, task-based and time-limited casework and structured groupwork.

The nature of knowledge for social work practice is contested, of course, and there is debate about the limitations of traditional research designs in a field where shared meanings are so important. However, it is clear that the absence of practitioner evaluation and of a culture of evaluation in social work have been serious obstacles to progress. The establishment of the Social Care Institute for Excellence will provide an increasingly sophisticated database of evidence about social work effectiveness. The General Social Care Council will provide the means for professional sanction. Social work has at last developed the super-structure of a profession after a long history of self-doubt and uncertainty.

The history of social work (part 2)

Four reports feature prominently in the post-war history of social work education in the UK. The first Carnegie report on the Employment and Training of Social Workers in the UK was published in 1947

(Younghusband 1947). It demonstrated a fragmented occupation, with chaotic arrangements for training, and a marked lack of attention to the integration of knowledge and skills. It was followed by the second Carnegie report (Younghusband 1951) which discussed further the identity of social work and set out a vision of what it was capable of becoming. It led to the establishment of generic applied social studies courses, and reinforced the arguments for an integrated social work profession based on social casework methods.

In 1968 the Seebohm Report pointed towards the establishment of integrated personal social services departments, which were to unify local authority social work services and social care provision, and to plan for total community needs. The departments created by the 1970 Social Services Act were to cover all service groups, and came to employ generically-trained social workers, although this was not Lord Seebohm's intention: his argument was primarily for generic departments. There were some voices in opposition to these developments. The Association of Metropolitan Authorities, for example, favoured separate childcare and mental health/welfare departments. Butrym (1976) suggested these changes undermined the opportunity to make social work an integral part of education and healthcare respectively, and questioned how such large departments could support social work as a professional enterprise focused on individuals. This was regarded as an eccentric and academic view at the time.

In 1982 the Barclay Report proposed wider use of social work teams attached to small areas in pursuit of better preventative work and better links with local communities. There was a debate about the application of this approach in areas without any prior community capacity and about the feasibility of doing statutory child protection whilst seeking to be engaged with the community. In the following decade, as demand grew, most Social Service Departments reduced the scale of their groupwork and community development activity.

In 1990 Sir Roy Griffiths published his report which led to the 1990 NHS and Community Care Act. This ushered in the mixed economy of social care and led to the establishment of care management as the predominent activity of social workers working with adults and older people. It prefigured a renewed emphasis on specialisms in social work departments and was associated with the emergence of the concept of competences in social work and social care practice. In relation to care management, it was soon made clear by the Department of Health that assessment and care planning could be done in multi-disciplinary teams and by professionals from other disciplines. Since these activities had often been seen as the unique preserve of social work (arguably leaving other skills in therapeutic work, rehabilitation and counselling relatively neglected), one common reaction from social workers was a sense of malaise. However, a more positive reaction was to emphasise what social workers could bring to multi-disciplinary and multi-agency settings: the social model of disability, respect for individual rights and self-determination, and what Smale *et al* called 'the joining skills' of empathy and authenticity which are at the heart of the professional relationship (Smale *et al*, 2000).

Social work training

The post-war history of social work training has been fragmented. From a handful of places in the 1950s (spread across child care and mental health, probation and health and welfare), the number of courses grew to over 120 by 1971 when the Central Council for Education and Training in Social Work was created to oversee the creation of a new single certificate, the CQSW. This generic qualification was intended to underpin a single profession, although this did not quite happen. Other staff in home care, day care and residential centres also needed training.

The Certificate in Social Services (CSS) was introduced to offer a shorter, more technical training based on workplace and agency needs. The CSS had many similarities with the most recent social work curriculum in its design and educational philosophy, and its later merger with social work training left a gap. Meanwhile, nursery nursing was beginning to extend its reach from daycare to home support with advanced family work courses appearing (Smith 1996). In due course the CQSW and CSS were replaced by the Diploma in Social Work. Six core competencies were introduced: to communicate and engage; promote and enable; assess and plan; intervene and provide services, work in organisations and develop professional competence. These competencies were to be applied in the workplace to agreed standards.

Competency based development was resisted at first because it seemed to undermine professional discretion and strengthen managerial control. In fact, it has proven to be an important step towards professional status. It is likely that competency based development will still be with us in 2020 and seen as a well-regarded approach to the development of skills, knowledge and values. We will (probably) be much more relaxed about it, and less inclined to see it as opposing either academic education or the application of professional intuition.

The emphasis on generic training in the early stages of social work has led the profession towards a strong focus on the knowledge, values and skills needed to work with clients. It has also meant the agency context has been down played. The partnerships between employers, academic departments and placement providers that support the new Diploma courses rebalance this emphasis. This trend is likely to continue in future. Employers will seek to influence if not determine the nature of training. The new occupational standards to be introduced this year are based on five key roles and thirteen work units. The hope is that training will provide a platform for professional education rather than diminish it: education is critical and reflective, and associated with the development of a 'professional self', as well as technical skills.

Half of the three year degree will be spent in practice. This need not mean giving up on academic standards, because practice placements will have to be better supported and demonstrate closer integration of evidence, practice skills and professional reflection. Student units will have to be developed to support 'the practicum'. Social workers will be assessed on their ability to manage change and deliver required outcomes, reflect social work value in their practice, communicate with users, carers and communities, to function in multi-disciplinary settings, to apply social work theory, and to apply skills, knowledge, research and analytical abilities to promote opportunities for service users. This is a demanding curriculum which will set out the expectations on professional social workers for the next decade and beyond, and it is still likely to be influential in 2020.

It is difficult to secure the right balance between generic and specialist knowledge and skill. Commentators have questioned whether social work courses can include everything that is necessary and challenged the idea of generic training when practice is being refocused around the specialisms of childcare, older and disabled people, mental health, learning disability and probation (Pinker 1994). Some suggest that specialism should be pursued at the post-qualification stage, along the lines of the American model (Papell 1996). Others argue it should be introduced earlier, providing the core competencies and basic levels of practical experience have been achieved. This question about social worth depth and specialist knowledge (the vertical question) has been thrown into sharp relief by the related question about joint training with other disciplines that deal with the same service group (the horizontal question).

There have been strong voices calling for common entry into applied social studies courses, with a unified curriculum for the first year, and subsequent specialisation into distinct pathways such as housing, social policy, youth and community work or social work. Others have widened the field of debate and argued for a common entry to psychiatric and learning disability nursing and social work. The argument against this approach is that students need an embryonic professional base before they specialise, and before they have to deal with the challenges of inter-disciplinary practice. For example, some nurses are advocating a generic nursing degree followed by specialisation, to replace the current pathways.

The problem with this point of view is that in a world of staff shortages, where specialisation by service group will be the organisational reality, postponing specialist training may be a costly mistake. Nursing currently involves a foundation period and then training and education in a specific branch, such as children, adults, learning disability or mental health. Despite these differences, the public still see nursing as one profession. Social Services employers may in the future be more prepared to sacrifice breadth and professional coherence for the sake of focus and organisational depth. The debates of the Milford Conference may be reopened in terms of specialist social work and social care pathways. They are even more likely to be raised in the context of integrated training across professional boundaries. As other disciplines have incorporated social care values and endorsed advocacy and human rights issues, so their distance from social work has diminished.

The proposition for 2020 is that the continued existence of separate professions with separate training schemes working closely with the same service groups, and with common competencies would be unnecessary and confusing for service users. The prediction is that professions will coalesce and merge to take the specialist path rejected at the Milford Conference. To the extent that there are serious staff shortages across related areas of the public services, this trend will accelerate.

Learning disabilities

In many respects, the field of learning disability has developed fastest and furthest in terms of joint training. There are now at least five joint training courses which combine social work and learning disability. Sims (2000) describes this development in terms of the emerging synthesis of competences and the integration of service models between nursing and social work that was associated with hospital re-provision programmes and the movement towards community living. Following the Jay Report (1979), it looked as if social services would have an exclusive lead role and the Certificate of Social Services was seen as the most appropriate qualification. There had been many inpatients whose needs were almost entirely social: for supported accommodation, family support, community day activity and leisure facilities, and above all for friendship. Social workers, resource centre staff and supported living teams were in a position to offer advocacy and support the new ordinary life philosophy more strongly than nurses who had been based in long stay hospitals. The revised 1982 curriculum for Learning Disability Nursing picked up the current of advocacy and social support, and was much more balanced than its predecessors. Joint Community Mental Handicap Teams emerged soon after and Mental Handicap Nursing moved a long way towards social work and social care.

This was followed by developments in the other direction. Changes in the population of those with a learning disability (for example more young people with multiple impairments and challenging behaviours, the identification of Alzheimers Disease as a significant issue for older people with Down's Syndrome and the emergence of Autism on a large scale) and the recognition that there were still significant unmet health needs supported the view that both health and social care were equally important in this field (Singh 1997).

The new joint courses that have developed more recently meet both nursing and social work requirements. They provide the Common Foundation programme for nursing, and the specialist branch training as one of the four nursing pathways. The common competency frameworks incorporate the UKCC Nursing Outcomes and CCETSW's 1995 Core Competitives for Social Work. The model used by South Bank University, for example, is built on a framework of eight core competences, which are very close to the new social work occupational standards. The graduates emerging from these courses are well-equipped to take up a wide variety of posts across health and social care, at exactly the time when joint planning and commissioning and integrated service delivery are developing rapidly. This is what service users and families have asked for, and the early signs are good.

The key question that follows from these developments is why there should continue to be two bodies awarding legitimate professional standing and two funding streams to pay for it. By 2020 we might expect this position to be rationalised.

A '2020 vision' in terms of learning disabilities might therefore include a single, unified profession, with one validating and supervisory body focused on clear values and the philosophy of citizenship, with staff skilled in counselling, care planning, education, housing support, behavioural support and relevant nursing tasks, working to integrate service users into the community and to provide appropriate support to them and their families.

Early years services

The field of early years also gives us some signposts for the future. In 1992, Pugh outlined the lack of strategy and cohesion in early years provision and training. Problems included low levels of funding, wide geographical variations, little parental choice, a lack of co-ordination and little agreement on a common vision. Social services nurseries were closing, to be replaced by family centres dealing with special needs and child protection, although even these were struggling to survive (Pugh 1992).

This landscape was changing by the third edition of Pugh's book in 2001. A more integrated national policy – the National Childcare Strategy – had begun to emerge, bringing with it increased investment in services for the under 4s and out-of-school provision. The Working Families Tax Credit was starting to help with childcare costs and more family-friendly workplace policies were being pursued. Early Years Development and Childcare Partnerships had been created in local authority areas and early excellence centres established to spread good practice. Workforce developments included the introduction of the Foundation Stage of early education (up to the end of the reception class) and the creation of the Early Years National Training

Organisation. Inspections from Education and Social Services had also been unified.

Although this represented a remarkable degree of investment and modernisation, some claimed it still fell short of a coherent early years policy (Moss 1999). Others highlighted continuing problems with early years training (Abbot and Hentry 2001) claiming it was still uneven and erratic, there was a shortage of trained staff and low levels of qualification, a bewildering range of qualifications, and a gap between the Teacher Training Agency and the Early Years National Training Organisation. In addition, early childhood studies degrees were not coherently integrated into professional training pathways, for example they were not accepted for entry to primary teacher training.

A number of recent developments have sought to address these problems. It has been suggested the most appropriate model for early years training is that of the climbing frame, not the ladder, with multiple levels of entry (Abbot and Henry 2001). The NVQ Level 4 in Early Years Care and Education (the highest level) was put in place in 2000, and will be the equivalent of one year of full time higher education. This has opened up the potential for a fast-track route into early years teaching. These developments reinforce enhanced professional standards and better training across a sector that has often been left at the bottom of social policy.

The 30 Early Excellence Centres may point the way forward over the coming years. These aim to integrate education and social care, offer extended day childcare, support families and provide parenting education, link to other services such as community health and social work, offer training for adults and spread good practice. It is unfortunate that only a few are based around primary schools, when the division between nursery and infant provision still appears to be more about professional convenience than the outcome of age-related and child centred practice.

The early years revolution that is taking place has huge potential to support emotional and cognitive development, social skills and health in young children, and to give parents support and opportunities for learning themselves. The 2020 vision for Early Years Services is one of comprehensive coverage for all children, extra help for the most disadvantaged, the professional climbing frame of training and education fully completed, and early years practitioners integrating within their professional identities the triple mantra of 'education, social care and health'. It is also a vision of new ways of working with parents and employers as partners.

Sure Start

Sure Start is a universal service for all children under 4 (and their carers) in the poorest localities. It seeks to improve social and emotional development, reduce child protection registrations, improve health, reduce the number of mothers smoking in pregnancy, improve children's ability to learn, reduce speech and language problems, strengthen families and communities and reduce parental unemployment. Sure Start aims to reach poor families and not necessarily dysfunctional families. The service is modeled on the experience of organisations like Barnados and the Thomas Coram Foundation which suggests that in order to prevent the social exclusion of children and young people, services need to focus on meeting parents needs in a non-stigmatising way.

Sure Start programmes are planned and run by partnership committees involving parents' representatives, voluntary organisations and statutory agencies. Different ways of working feature in different Sure Start schemes, but all have a multi-agency focus. For example, Euston Sure Start has an outreach team of workers from eight different agencies, all working to the same job description and all linked back to their parent agencies. Isolated families can be visited at home and provided with practical help with child behaviour and relationship problems. Families are also encouraged to take part in activities designed by parents for parents, and in education and training.

Sure Start is subject to a long-term evaluation. So far, there is evidence that participants enjoy the programmes and do not feel stigmatised using them. However, a number of challenges are beginning to emerge. Firstly, whilst Sure Start services are available to all families in the area, they are not universally used. Further research is need as to why this is the case. Secondly, there is anecdotal evidence that referrals to Social Services are rising significantly as hidden need and risk is uncovered. Statutory services may not be sufficiently resourced to deal with this unmet need. Thirdly, including some of the most vulnerable families ('those who need it but don't want it', according to Naomi Eisenstadt, Sure Start's National Director) is proving difficult.

There is a serious concern that the limited funding of mainstream services could disrupt the progress of Sure Start. This is not a new problem. In the 1990s, funding shortages and the rising pressure on child protection work, residential placements and help for disabled children deflected many social services and community family centres from a universal ethos, leading them to concentrate on the most dysfunctional families. For things to be different this time round, Sure Start needs proper funding, which ought not to be secured at the expense of child protection or more therapeutically orientated services for very damaged children such as health visitors, housing officers and social workers who are already overloaded in providing local services.

Despite these challenges, Sure Start appears to have considerable potential for improving the lives of disadvantaged children. A key factor is its empowering and emancipatory model. Professionals have to work alongside parents who have a say in the governance of the service, its design and programme management. They have to balance their professional backgrounds and agency loyalty with this ethos (a challenge which, at least so far, seems to be being met). Sure Start raises interesting questions about the links between parents (as service users, volunteers and employers) and professionals.

Empowerment and partnership are easy to espouse in theory, and difficult to implement in practice. The great hope of Sure Start is that parental and community involvement in decision-making will give the programmes a strength and efficacy that has so far been missing. The vision for 2020 is that ethically sound, evidence-based programmes for young children and their families will be available in all poor neighbourhoods, designed and led by local parents with professional support as required.

The Connexions service

The Connexions service was introduced to tackle the problem of thousands of school leavers going missing from the education and training systems each year. Connexions provides an integrated service for all 13 to18 year olds during their transition through education and into work, with extra help and advocacy for those in the greatest need.

Its purpose is to raise aspirations, participation and achievement levels of all young people by providing a coherent, integrated and comprehensive set of services. This includes important information, advice and guidance opportunities for personal development, engagement in learning and other support to assist young people to make the successful transition to adult life.

The creation of Connexions has required the redesign and integration of many existing service functions in new combinations. The service is delivered by Personal Advisers who are drawn from a variety of backgrounds including careers, youth and community work, teaching, social work and counselling. They have six primary functions including engaging young people and supporting them in their personal development and learning; engaging with and influencing other agencies; developing and managing the provision of opportunities and support; ethical practices including equal opportunities and continuing professional development; and managing resources and supporting successful development and delivery.

It is interesting to note the high degree of overlap with social work and social care, for example engaging with and responding to young people and their concerns, facilitating access to and support for learning, personal development, employment and leisure opportunities, monitoring and reviewing progress with young people and engaging with parents, carers and families. It is likely that this overlap will lead to the development of a competency framework with a high degree of commonality with social work and social care. Some moves in this direction are already taking place, such as the level 2 undergraduate course, the Diploma for Connexion Personal Advisers, which has been designed jointly with the Youth Justice Board.

The evolution of Connexions Personal Advisers will probably lead to the creation of a new profession for supporting teenagers. This profession will in part fill the niche that is covered on the continent by 'social educators'. Since the training for residential childcare is constrained by limitations within the Diploma in Social Work, a 2020 vision would see a unified profession being established to provide staff for youth and community work settings, social work teams, youth justice services, teenage health promotion, adolescent mental health services, residential homes, foyer schemes, adolescent careers services and Connexions.

Youth offending teams

There have been major changes in the youth justice system in England and Wales, related to the establishment of the Youth Offending Teams (YOTs). The White Paper 'No More Excuses' (Home Office, 1997) highlighted the need for earlier intervention and risk management and The Youth Justice Board for England and Wales was established in 1998 to implement new policies and practices as a matter of urgency.

The focus was on close inter-agency working, and providing local leadership through a board and a youth offending team manager. Objectives, performance measures, protocols and professional tools have been supplied from the Youth Justice Board and individual YOTs have the task of joining these up locally with other agencies and the local community.

Youth offending teams have seconded staff from probation, social services, health, housing, education and the youth service. They have also recruited new staff directly to the teams. Tasks are closely defined, for example supervising a child after custody, running a youth offender panel, completing an assessment (ASSET), recommending a referral order, and dealing with final warnings. Methods of intervention include one-to-one counselling, group activities, parental support, liaison with schools and colleges, and links with the welfare-to-work programmes. As the new Connexions Service is rolled out nationally, there will be strong links required with Youth Justice.

YOT members come from a wide variety of backgrounds and bring with them a diverse range of skills and experience. Training and development has been a major concern, in terms of teambuilding and the establishment of core competencies. The Youth Justice Board's training programme for operational managers will provide a framework for managing the service, and front-line training will follow. The YOT should not follow the recent example of the Probation Service by becoming too focused on a narrow range of indicators and running the risk of neglecting child development and core counselling skills, thereby detaching itself from wider initiatives for teenagers. The 2020 vision is therefore of a service which considers the whole life of young offenders and is underpinned by integrated training for YOTs along with Connexions, Youth and Community Services, Social Services.

Some other developments

A range of other developments could have important implications for the future social care workforce. For example, it is interesting to note the discovery by the psychiatric disciplines of the psychosocial model of intervention in mental health and the value of multidisciplinary teamwork (including employment support and housing) for people with serious and enduring conditions. The application of the social model in mental health could have major consequences for the education and training of mental health practitioners in future. The key question is whether closer integration between health and social care will undermine the social model of disability as it applies to mental health.

The Government's aspiration towards integrated services for older people will require more professional flexibility. If function shapes form, by 2020 there will be multi-skilled rehabilitation and support teams with staff drawn from a range of disciplines including nursing, occupational therapy, social work and home support. At some point, as a result of demographic pressure if nothing else, we might expect to see the creation of an occupation or profession drawing elements from all these disciplines focusing on older people. Dementia care, in particular, will require the equivalent of assertive outreach teams, and these will need to incorporate the positive approaches of both the social disability models and the hospice traditions. Other agencies may also emerge to support the UK's aging population. For example, 'Finance and Care' agencies could introduce sophisticated financial products to help people use their resources better in later life, as house prices rise further over the coming decades.

Information and communication technologies could have a profound impact on service delivery and professional practice. Telematics has the potential to make life easier for service users and carers in areas such as controlled living environments, shopping and communications (Tetley *et al* 2000). Intelligent information systems will suggest options for care planning and assessment (including the assessment of risk) which are supported by evidence. This will free up social workers for more face-to-face contact and the direct use of their core therapeutic skills. Information Management Technology specialists are likely to be regular contributors to professional training programmes in health and social care in future, helping practitioners become skilled at using these new electronic tools.

The use of new technologies could also help overcome fragmentation and poor communications. Electronic Care records may be widely used by 2020, linked to both patient and educational records. There will be close attention to the elaboration of typical pathways of care. The potential can already be seen in embryonic developments such as the electronic social care record created in Leeds and in the evidence from Bradford Social Services and software developers Liquid Logic to the Climbié Enquiry which supported a virtual 'real time' chronology of home visits. A new discipline of health and social care informatics could develop to map out changing patterns of need at the local level and support key decision-makers with intelligent systems. The capability to do all of these things already exists today. As their use spreads, staff will need to develop the knowledge and skills to deal with the world of e:Care.

Conclusion

The world of 2020 could see social work as we know it dissolved into its constituent functions and competencies, and redistributed across the map of new initiatives. Generic social work practice and training could fade away, to be replaced by more specialised and focused developments based around the newly emerging 'social exclusion' professions and the newly integrated agencies. Hybrid occupations will almost certainly emerge, incorporating elements from several existing professions.

However, against these trends the strength of the new social work degree will exert pressure to keep social work intact. This could be achieved in a number of ways. The development of specialised pathways in social work and social care, and of joint training and education with other professions, need not be seen as the end of social work but as the next chapter in an evolving story. After all, nursing has a common identity despite the divisions within it and the very different settings in which it is practiced. The interesting question is the extent to which social work and social care will stand their ground in the new agencies and prove to be of value to them. They will do this best by serving people well, building on social care values and skills, and making a full contribution to both management and practice development.

Social care and social work practitioners will demand better training and education in future. Personal development opportunities will be a vital key to future recruitment, as will comparative salary levels. A range of other questions remain to be addressed. Can we envisage a large differential within social work and across the new agencies to secure the services of experienced child protection staff with advanced qualifications? Do we need social work consultants who merit senior standing? Should this work be done in local authorities or do we need a new agency for children?

Child protection is only a small part of the work of Social Service Departments, and depends much on the work of others, especially health visitors, teachers, doctors and the police. However, the current organisational fragmentation does not support good practice for children. A crucial element of any vision for 2020 is that genuinely effective multi-disciplinary child protection teams are in place, with child protection investigation a valued activity given all the help it needs. This vision also includes readily available treatment for abused children and support for their birth families (if the family is intact and safe) and for adoptive and foster parents. There are strong arguments in favour of an integrated children and families service incorporating specialist child protection teams, community health services, social work and social care, child and adolescent mental health services, child psychology and special educational services for children with educational needs that require help beyond the classroom.

This chapter has argued for a wide definition of social work and social care. It has not dealt with the issue of public accountability. Local government has been enriched by its responsibility for the services outlined above, and the link has reinforced the position of service users as citizens. It will be important that the new agencies should be participatory and accountable in their governance. In all these changes, the vision remains of good quality personal services, supported by a strong social mandate, built on personal relationships and trust, respecting human rights and empowerment. Or as some put it: 'organisations with a heart' (Kouzos and Posner 1999).

Bibliography

AASW (1929) *Milford Conference Proceedings* American Association of Social Work

Abbot L and Hevey D (2001) 'Training to work in the early years: developing the climbing frame' in Pugh G (2001) *Contemporary issues in the early years: working collaboratively for children* Paul Chapman

Butrym Z (1976) *The Nature of Social Work* Macmillan

Etzioni A (1969) *The Semi-professions and their Organization* Free Press

Freidson E (1970) *Profession of Medicine* Dodd/Mead.

Gilchrist R and Jeffs T (2001) *Settlements, Social Action and Social Change* Jessica Kingsley.

Home Office (1997) *No More Excuses: a new approach to tackling youth crime in England and Wales* The Stationery Office

Jay P (1979) *Report of the Committee of Inquiry into Mental Handicap Nursing and Care* HMSO

Jordan B and Jordan C (2000) *Social Work and the Third Way* London: Sage

Kouzos J and Posner P (1999) *Encouraging the Heart* Wiley

McDonald G and Sheldon B (1992) 'Contemporary Studies of the Effectiveness of Social Work' *British Journal of Social Work* 22.6

Moss P (1999) 'Renewed Hopes and Lost Opportunities: early childhood in the early years of the Labour Government' *Cambridge Journal of Education* 29

Munro E (1998) *Understanding Social Work* Athlone Press

Papell C (1996) 'Reflections on issues in social work education' in Gould N and Taylor I (eds) (1996) *Reflective Learning for Social Work* Arena

Payne M (1996) *What is Professional Social Work?* Venture Press

Pinker B (1994) 'Devil's advocate' *Community Care* 24-30 November 1994

Pugh G (ed) (1992) *Contemporary Issues in the Early Years: working collaboratively for children* Paul Chapman

Pugh G (ed) (1991) *Contemporary Issues in the Early Years: working collaboratively for children* Paul Chapman

Richmond M (1917) *Social Diagnosis* Russell Sage Foundation

Sims, D (2000) 'The Joint Practitioner – A New Identity' in Harris J, Froggett and Paylor (eds) (2000) *Reclaiming Social Work: The Southport Papers* Venture/BASW.

Singh P (1997) *Prescription for Change* Mencap

Smale G, Tuson G and Statham D (2000) *Social work and social problems: working towards social inclusion and social change* Basingstoke: Macmillan

Smith T (1996) *Family Centres and Bringing up Young Children* London: HMSO

Tetley J *et al* (2000) 'Older people, telematics and care' in Warner A (ed) (2000) *Care Services for Later Life* Jessica Kingsley

Warner A (eds) (2000) *Care Services for Later Life* Jessica Kingsley

Wilensky H (1963) 'The Professionalization of Everbody' *American Journal of Society* 70

Younghusband E (1951) *Social work in Britain: a supplementary report on the employment and training of social workers* Carnegie United Kingdom Trust

Younghusband E (1947) *Report on the employment and training of social workers* T & A Constable

5. Structures and accountability

Anne Davies

Chapters 2, 3 and 4 have looked at the long term future of social care from three different standpoints: changing demand, aims and objectives, and workforce issues. This chapter considers structural and accountability issues. Which institutional forms will be appropriate for social care in ten to twenty years' time?

Since the inception of the welfare state, social care has experienced many institutional changes. Elements have moved between local government and national agencies, principally the National Health Service, and between statutory, private and voluntary sectors, demonstrating that social care is viable in different settings. However, the locus of responsibility for social care has been local government. It has therefore evolved in a culture of local democracy and it is now difficult to separate concerns about the future of social care from those of local government itself.

Social care is also a national service, paid for out of general taxation. This means that the way social care responsibilities are distributed and organised is a matter for negotiation between central and local government. Political leadership is thus a key factor.

This chapter presents an overview of present structural and accountability aspects of social care, which is experiencing rapid change and an uncertain future. It also offers two hypotheses for the longer term, one which anticipates a bigger role at the regional level of government, and one scenario in which social care and health are jointly commissioned within a democratic framework. These are not presented as the likely culmination of present trends – rather the reverse – but for the purpose of stimulating debate.

Terminology

The subject under discussion is social care as a function, as distinct from social services and social work. Social care, as discussed in the previous chapters, is not embodied in any one service but refers to the function of supporting people to live independent lives. Nor is it confined to any one context. It embraces not only the role of social workers, but also a range of other professions.

Since the Local Authority Social Services Act of 1970, councils have a statutory responsibility for social care which they have traditionally discharged through social services departments (SSDs). The term 'social services' is usually a reference to these departments. They inherited many of the functions of local government children's departments and welfare departments, which had grown out of Poor Law institutions. Each council is also required by the same 1970 Act to appoint a Director of Social Services.

Social work refers to the process of providing interpersonal care and support. Professional social workers currently comprise less than ten per cent of the workforce of Social Services Departments. They operate from various settings in the public, voluntary and private sectors. Like most professions, social workers are an identifiable group by virtue of their common values and skills, rather than their organisation.

Public service accountability

In a democracy, it is axiomatic that a public service such as social care, which is authorised in statute and publicly funded, must be accountable. This is in order to assess competence, to ensure financial probity, to safeguard administrative propriety and to guarantee responsiveness (on the grounds that there is no point in delivering a service no-one either needs or wants). Neither political nor financial accountability is attainable without the necessary powers to hold an organisation to account and to act upon it. Although the process of accountability relies on scrutiny, that is not, in itself sufficient. As John Stewart has pointed out, an accountable relationship can only exist when those to whom an account is given can exercise direct sanctions over those who are accountable (Chartered Institute of Public Finance and Accountancy 1998). There is thus a difference between accountability and responsibility, where an account may be given, but no sanctions exist. The traditional way of achieving public accountability is through democracy, which obtains a mandate for public action through periodic elections. However flawed this may be, no better alternative has been found. A variety of measures can be used to augment democracy, such as public consultations, scrutiny rights and the involvement of user groups, but they cannot in themselves provide an adequate substitute.

The degree of accountability required for a public service will be a formative influence on its structure. Where accountability is built into the structure, it will permeate the whole culture of the organisation and establish its relationship with the public. In a public service like social care, which sometimes treads a fine line between care and control, this relationship is vital.

A public service is accountable to the user, who has rights enforceable in law, and to the public or citizenry which pays for, and effectively owns the service and which determines the policies. Public services like social care and health increasingly aim to customise their services to fit the user and, as John McTernan argues in his chapter, are becoming more individualist where once they were collectivist and more pluralistic as they emphasise choice. Correspondingly, concepts of rights to services have supplanted those of needs, which were the basis of the original welfare state, and this in turn has tended to downplay the collective ownership aspect of public services. Accountability is increasingly directed towards the consumer or user rather than to the citizen. However inexorable its rise, the consumerist model does not easily extend to social care because most people do not regard themselves as even potential users of social care, and others who use it have no choice, as for example in child protection.

In John Stewart's analysis of public service accountability there are professional, economic, legal and democratic dimensions. Responsibility for the first three is distributed between a range of institutions at the central government level, auditing, inspecting and adjudicating, whereas democratic accountability can only be obtained at the local level. Sheer distance, force of numbers and lack of detailed knowledge make it impossible for central government to hold local institutions to account. Social care, which is, of its very essence, a local service must be accountable at the local level.

Social services departments have been locally accountable since their establishment in 1970. The decision to municipalise social care was made on the recommendations of the Seebohm Committee which reported in 1968. It was a departure from the structures devised for other welfare services, including health, which relied exclusively on the centralising ministerial model of accountability, as did nationalised industries and a whole range of public bodies which were made accountable nationally, through ministers, to Parliament. Social services departments were established in local authorities partly to separate social care from a medically dominated NHS. This separation was accentuated when, in 1974, responsibility for public health and a variety of community health services was taken out of local government and merged into the NHS. Thirty years later the nature of the relationship between social care and health still dominates the question of how social care should be organised.

Issues of central-local government relations hinge on finding an acceptable balance between central and local accountability and between uniformity and autonomy. This became seriously one-sided in favour of central government during the 1980s and early 1990s with the introduction of compulsory competitive tendering to local government and substantial reductions in their role as direct providers of housing and education. Rate-capping further curtailed local autonomy. Local councils came to be perceived by central government less as democratically elected leaders of their communities and more as local outposts of central government or units of administration.

An alternative view argued that local authorities should become the expression of communities governing themselves – the basic unit of community government. This would require 'a strategic role for an enabling local authority; responsiveness in service delivery and a renewed basis for accountability' (Stewart and Stoker 1988) a vision which informed present Government policy on local government. The Local Government Act 2000 placed a duty on local authorities to produce community strategies with new powers to improve and promote economic, social and environmental wellbeing. Other initiatives are intended to revitalise local democracy including new formats for councils, alternatives to traditional committees, the possibility of elected mayors and a range of measures to improve levels of participation in local elections. Present government policy also recognises the importance of citizenship, which not only gives validity to the actions of representative democracy but is also a necessary component of caring communities. The drive to rebuild an active, participatory democracy at the local level must be sustained because a future in which local communities have no democratic voice or political expression is difficult, if not impossible to envisage.

A national programme of neighbourhood renewal relies on the development of local strategic partnerships and the piloting of local public service agreements. These place central-local government relations on a contractual basis so that local authorities commit themselves to delivering key national and local priorities in return for agreed flexibilities, pump priming funding and financial rewards.

The current emphasis on local government's strategic role, the importance of partnership, the revitalisation of local democracy and the regeneration of communities are four elements of policy which strengthen local government's claim to be the appropriate setting for a publicly accountable social care service.

However, funding is a key factor in the structuring of an accountable public service, and social care is funded from national taxation. As long ago as 1976, the Layfield Committee expressed concern about the growth in central funding provided to local authorities. At that time two thirds of resources came from the centre which, Layfield argued, undermined local accountability. The Committee proposed a local income tax which was not introduced and by 2001/02, the proportion of central government funding for local authorities had increased to three quarters (Stoker and Travers 2001). Since 1990, when the business rate was abolished to make way for the short-lived poll tax, there have been repeated but unsuccessful calls for its restoration. Stoker and Travers argue that since Layfield, the central task of local government has been redefined:

> We have moved from an era where local government was delineated by its capacity to provide a discrete set of services as required by its local residents to one where the key responsibility of local government is to steer or guide its communities towards desired local outcomes. We have moved from an era of traditional local government to the wider sphere of 'governance' (Stoker and Travers 2001).

This trend is reflected in social care, where social services departments now function in the context of a mixed economy of providers and their key role is in commissioning services, stipulating outcomes and providing public accountability.

If local tax raising powers were to be introduced they would be too limited to make an impact on social care budgets. Central funding will inevitably continue, so accountability for overall policy and for public expenditure must be provided through Parliament, but in a way that is compatible with democratic accountability for the delivery of local services. This is a dichotomy with which local government is familiar and it may not be cynical to suggest that any confusion in the public mind about who is responsible for what can be convenient to government in the event of service failure. Local authorities are also able to attribute culpability to the government for funding shortages.

John McTernan argues that in a 'post ideological age', politicians must give priority to delivering high quality public services, which focus on the end-user, deliver choice and generally respond to individual demand. This is difficult within the relative rigid framework of central or national accountability. The political institutions and constitutional conventions used to deliver accountability to the voter and tax-payer, are also ineffectual and ill-suited to the management of public services. Witness the inadequacy of ministerial responsibility, a conspicuously inefficient Parliament, the sidelined select committees, which are the chief agents of scrutiny in the House of Commons, and a near-moribund upper House. The political side of the accountability equation demonstrably fails to deliver, but it continues to be a major influence on structures, particularly in relation to the NHS where managers have a metaphorical crick in their necks from looking upwards to Government, rather than outwards towards patients.

Central control or local autonomy?

The lack of local accountability has caused problems for the NHS since 1947, and there have been repeated attempts to compensate by establishing links with local councils. However, governments have been ambivalent in their commitment to a municipal role. The Thatcher government removed local authority representation from health authorities and restructured them along private boardroom lines. When issues of 'rationing' became controversial as in the so-called 'Child B case', it was all too evident that the lack of genuine accountability made it impossible to devolve major ethical decisions to unelected health authorities.

The present government has introduced a variety of measures to involve local authorities in health and has gone so far as to give them a power of scrutiny over local health bodies. It has also restored some rights to representation on boards, and set up an elaborate set of new institutions to represent the patient. These include Patients Advice and Liaison Services in every trust along with Patients Forums which can nominate a representative to be non executive directors on trust boards, an independent Complaints Advocacy Service and the national Commission for Patient and Public Involvement in Health. Local authority Overview and Scrutiny Committees have powers to scrutinise local health services and 'call NHS managers to account' (Department of Health 2001a).

The pressure for central accountability – for national rather than local services – comes not only from the top down but from public expectations of equity. Where once it was acceptable, local autonomy is now challenged when it leads to significant disparities. The 'postcode lottery' in service provision is widely considered unacceptable and is an influential factor in present policy to tackle health inequalities and social exclusion. It provides a rationale for centralised, national structures and generates substantial pressure for uniformity in the quality of services between localities and hence curtailment of local accountability. On the other hand, public services like social care are intended to be flexible and responsive to need, so there must be in-built capacity for variation. This presents a dilemma. The established method of mitigating inequitable results of local autonomy is the setting of national standards enforceable through inspection, and this has been an integral and formative element in the development of social services provision. More recently excessive demands for conformity to centrally prescribed procedures and outcomes have culminated in the publication of performance league tables of which social services star ratings are the latest. Paradoxically greater conformity is rewarded with 'earned autonomy' – presumably a freedom to do things differently.

The impact of this audit explosion was the subject of the 2002 Reith Lectures by Onora O'Neill who commented on the damage to professionalism in health, education and social work: 'Each profession has its proper aim, and this is not reducible to meeting set targets following prescribed procedures and requirements... The new accountability is widely experienced not just as changing, but I think as distorting the proper aims of professional practice and indeed as damaging professional pride and integrity'.

This effect is noticeable in social care and in the NHS, both of which are within the remit of the Department of Health. A recent editorial in the British Medical Journal referred to 'unprecedented micro-management from the centre, which has the effect of constraining and undermining the ability of managers to manage... They (ministers) display an unforgiving, top down command and control style of management (partly a reflection of the lack of trust and respect) in which unrealistic targets and objectives are showered down on managers, who are left feeling undermined and undervalued' (Smith, Walsh and Hunter 2001).

An alternative is to find ways of devolving decision-making to locally accountable bodies, creating a better balance between central control and local autonomy. Realistically, accountability mechanisms at the national level must be confined to broad policy direction, and to financial accountability to ensure that public money has been properly spent (these are matters for audit and Parliamentary scrutiny). Accountability for the delivery of the service has to take place at the local level. This presupposes greater local freedoms in matters of service delivery.

Ultimately, finding the right balance between local autonomy and equity is a matter for political decisions. For example, the decision to devolve powers to the Scottish Parliament enabled social care policy on Scotland to deviate from policy in England and Wales by removing charging for personal care services. The question of whether this is fair or equal treatment for people in Scotland compared with England is really a question about sovereignty; the decision may lead to increased equity or fairness within Scotland.

Governance of social care

In addition to considerations of accountability, the institutional form taken by social care must follow from the functions it performs. Gerald Wistow has argued in this book, how structures and processes are logically subordinate to values, principles and desired outcomes.

Present Government policy as set out in 'Modernising Social Services' (Department of Health 1998) aims to provide a universal social care service on the grounds that each of us will, at some point in our lives, need it for ourselves or our families. The Secretary of

State for Health, Alan Milburn has described his vision of an 'active welfare state' promoting independence and prosperity through the creation of social as well as economic opportunities for all people. Social care is seen, in this view, as a 'liberating force' consistent with the vision of social care described with such prescience in the Seebohm Report of 1968.

Gerald Wistow suggests that the purpose of social care is to maximise the wellbeing of individuals, their networks, communities and wider society. He also argues that, whatever the structures, the following social services tasks and functions will remain to be fulfilled: empowering vulnerable people; supporting autonomous decision making; mobilising community resources; developing care networks; promoting wellbeing and primary prevention; advocating integrated services and integrated accountability; promoting holistic governance to meet the holistic needs of individuals in their community (Wistow 2001). The concept of interdependence is formative, as is the need to build strong and supportive communities.

The accountability which local authorities can deliver to their communities creates a framework for the governance of social care as responsive, integrated and holistic services which recognise the interdependence of people. Moreover, communities, families and individuals are more likely to accept and value social care, particularly interventions in highly sensitive areas such as child protection or mental health, if there is some sense of common ownership and mutual benefit. The authority which social care must have cannot depend on the force of law but is instead derived from its democratic legitimacy, its 'connectedness' to the community it serves.

This analysis suggests not only that a democratic local authority provides the appropriate framework of governance in which to deliver social care, it goes further and implies that social care and local government have become inter-dependent. This is firstly, because both now pursue the same goal of individual and collective wellbeing, and, secondly, because each needs the other to achieve that goal. The argument is thus not whether local government should be responsible for social care – it should – but in what institutional forms it will ensure its delivery. The next section in this chapter explores some of the options.

Structures

Social care is organised in ever more disparate and complex ways and is in a period of transition. In his chapter, Liam Hughes suggests that social work in the future could be 'redistributed across the map of new social initiatives'. It will increasingly work across many boundaries, not only with the NHS but the police, education, probation, housing, youth work and so on. New ways of working in multi-disciplinary contexts are being developed which do not rely on structural reform. Government policy needs to allow scope for organisational change to take place in response to local circumstances.

Consideration of social care structures, whether in relation to new initiatives or the reorganisation of existing institutions, must take account of some basic principles. Structures and organisations are not an end in themselves but a means to an end. Skills and capacity are often as, if not more, important. There must be clearly understood reasons why one structure is chosen over another. It should also be acknowledged that removing one set of boundaries may simply create another set. Restructuring carries a cost: services may suffer, there may be confusion for the user; staff may become de-motivated, jobs may lost and there may be administrative costs. Structures may be right but processes and implementation defective. Structures need time and favourable conditions to demonstrate their effectiveness. Ultimately it is less important that existing organisations should last, than that social care values should endure and care be provided when and where it is needed.

Removing structural obstacles

It could be argued that the consideration of new structures should be delayed until present obstacles to improving service delivery have been addressed. The Tenth Annual Report of the Chief Inspector of Social Services drew attention to some of the problems currently facing service providers. Recruitment and retention of appropriately qualified staff was identified as the most serious issue, accompanied by poor public image, particularly of social workers as projected by the media. Staff shortages are particularly acute in children's services (Department of Health 2001b).

The report points to a number of obstacles which might be amenable to immediate change. For example, the lack of co-ordination between the budgetary processes of the NHS and local authorities currently 'severely impairs joint planning and joint investment in pooled budgets'. Poor information sharing is another issue. According to the report, the NHS was unable to supply full information about delayed discharges in 26 per cent of council areas. A similar percentage received inadequate or no information about hospital emergency admissions. Complex and changing planning requirements which are intended to facilitate a joined up approach are also 'getting in the way of coherent service delivery rather than improving it'.

The report also identified budget pressures, lack of resources and the impact of increasing demand and overspends by councils as problems. These issues were the subject of recommendations in a recent report from the King's Fund which urged the government to recognise 'significant under-investment in care and support services' and recommended an order of investment at least the same as that being injected into the NHS: a growth of one third in real terms in the next five years (King's Fund 2001).

Finally, it is worth reflecting that the whole dynamic of the social care/NHS interface would shift if the charging regime for personal care were changed or, as in the case of Scotland, abolished.

Social services departments

Social services departments provide social care as well as commissioning an increasing amount (over 80 per cent) from the care 'market' of voluntary organisations and independent providers. The local authority remains accountable for those services by having a contract or accountability agreement with each provider. SSDs are comparable to primary care trusts in the NHS, in that both are providers and commissioners of services. It is also part of the function of SSDs to contribute to the many strategies which local authorities must produce.

An increasing volume of social care is being delivered outside SSDs by means of central government initiatives such as Sure Start and Connexions, all of which have their own structures and boundaries, and their own governance arrangements. Some, like Sure Start attach considerable importance to developing user involvement. Collectively, the expansion of these agencies has undermined the public accountability traditionally obtained through Directors of Social Services who are in the unenviable position of being held responsible for social care, while their authority and influence has been eroded (Department of Health 2000).

A substantial part of the task of SSDs is to work in partnership with a whole range of other organisations, of which the NHS is one. They are now under intense pressure from government policy to integrate specific services within the NHS. There is a further challenge in the possibility of a government initiative which would introduce a new structure to take over child protection services. Either development would have a profound impact; taken together they would entirely change the function of social services departments.

Bearing in mind the basic principles which should govern considerations of structure, several options are now explored.

Care trusts

The need to overcome boundary problems between NHS and social care is a major objective of current health policy, particularly in relation to services for older people, and problems cased by 'bed-blocking' in hospitals. The concept of Care Trusts was introduced in the Health and Social Care Act 2001. In essence, they will take social care responsibilities out of local government and into the NHS as specially created devolved local bodies with a unified board of management. They use the flexibilities provided by Section 31 of the 1999 Health Act, to pool budgets, delegate leads and integrate services. According to the Secretary of State: 'reform will mean giving patients what they need – one care system, not two' (*The Guardian* 2002).

Arguably social care professionals could interpret care trusts as an opportunity to extend their sphere of influence into health. Unfortunately, the care trust model on offer does not provide a level playing field. Care trusts are not partnerships operating at arm's length from local authorities and the NHS. The Health and Social Care Act specifies that they will be NHS bodies. Moreover, the first trusts have been set up voluntarily, but the Secretary of State has powers (under section 46 of the Act) to direct authorities to enter into delegation or pooled fund arrangements. This has not yet been tested and the view from those working within care trusts suggests such a direction would be inoperable, since care trusts are best seen as a stage in partnership working, and can only be built on existing collaboration. Nevertheless, government policy, as articulated by the Secretary of State, appears to place considerable emphasis on their development: 'Joint working must become the norm for all and not just for some. The powers to pool budgets and to form care trusts so that health and social care functions are merged must be taken up' (*The Guardian* 2002).

Care trusts have raised numerous concerns, not only about accountability, but also the threat they present to social care values: the fear that the holistic view, which takes account of the individual within their family and community setting, will be submerged by the medical culture which dominates the NHS. This is of particular concern to older people and to disabled people who have fought long and hard to escape the patient role and implement a social model of disability (*The Guardian* 2001a). Other commentators have supported this view:

> If the new battle were about saving departmental boundaries it would not be worth fighting…. Putting care trusts under the NHS would be disastrous. Just look at geriatric services: poor status, few resources. Elderly people are the bottom of NHS priorities. Worse still, community care would regress from being a social and medical service to purely medical (*The Guardian* 2001b).

The Association of Directors of Social Services has opposed care trusts, largely for the reasons already referred to, and also on the grounds that there is no 'one-size fits all' model of care. In fact, the first Care Trusts to be set up differ in terms of the responsibilities delegated to them and the structures they have adopted. The unifying factor is that all are NHS bodies. Broadly speaking, there are provider care trusts, which have no commissioning function, like Camden, which has adopted the NHS trust model. There are also provider and commissioning care trusts, like Northumberland, which have adopted the NHS Primary Care Trust model and which is closest to the original concept set out by the Department of Health. Somerset has opted for another version: a dual structure with a care trust provider and a separate joint commissioning board which handles commissioning, monitoring and evaluation.

Responsibility for specific social care services is delegated to a care trust by the local authority thereby reducing the accountability framework to a largely contractual one. Usually there is a one year notice break clause to reverse the agreement. Staff and budgets, including the statutory responsibility of the council to collect social care charges, are delegated to the care trust. It has been suggested that care trusts offer a way for the NHS to lever in additional funding, such as Single Regeneration Budget funds, or access to councils' loan raising power.

Governance of care trusts is conducted by a NHS-style board with councillors from the local authority appointed as non-executive members. Thereafter the local authority has the same scrutiny rights which it exercises in relation to ordinary PCTs. Councillors on the board (in the case of Northumberland two from the ruling party on the council and one from the opposition) are nominated by the council and appointed by the NHS appointments commission along with other non-executive members. They are expected to act not as delegates from the local council but as corporate managers of the care trust, in the interests of the trust.

According to this model of governance, democratic accountability is reduced to scrutiny powers. It is theoretically possible that, following sustained under-performance or mismanagement by a care trust, or by the social care elements within it, or malpractice in the handling of the social care budget, the council could seek withdrawal from the care trust. Or, after the required period of notice, seek to reinstate some kind of direct management or make changes to the contract. In view of the Secretary of State's considerable powers of direction, this could ultimately be a matter for legal challenge.

Earlier, the point was made about a necessary trade off between the accountability and the effectiveness of a public service. Care trusts may offer one way forward, at a cost to democratic accountability, if they demonstrably provide an effective solution to the NHS/social care interface problem where alternative, accountable structures fail.

So far, only one care trust – Somerset – has been the subject of any research and the earliest results are not encouraging. Somerset Partnership Health and Social Care Trust was set up in 1999 to provide mental health services, in conjunction with a parallel joint commissioning board (set up by the county council and four Primary Care Groups) for mental health services. The two year evaluation, undertaken by the

Institute for Applied Health and Social Policy at Kings College London, found that joint commissioning and provision of mental health services in Somerset had failed to produce significant benefits to users over its first two years. Users considered access to services had deteriorated and concerns remained that there was no alternative to hospital admission in crises. Whilst users and carers were included as non-voting members of the commissioning board, users felt less involved in care planning than they had done before (Peck *et al* 2001).

The authors of the research reported that by the end of the evaluation they remained unsure whether the Trust had delivered anything which had not been delivered elsewhere without the transfer of social care staff to a new employer. They advised 'Learn from Somerset but don't copy it. Significant change is best home-grown' (Peck *et al* 2002).

The inspiration for the concept of care trusts would seem to be the Northern Ireland model, when, as Gerald Wistow has already pointed out, research there now suggests that the benefits are far from clear. In short, the evidence base for transferring social care into NHS trusts is not in place.

Options for the future development of Care Trusts are the subject of considerable debate. The Government has announced that, as part of its plans to decentralise power, high performing Trusts can become not for profit organisations (NFPs) with 'Foundation' status. Attention has so far focused on Foundation hospitals. However, the potential for Care Trusts and Primary Care Trusts (see below) to become NFPs has also been raised. The concept of 'public interest companies' is also attracting notice. Some commentators have suggested that Care Trusts could be a precursor to US-style health maintenance organisations (Webster 2002).

Although care trusts have been set up in limited areas of social care, their development as an integrated health and social care model is a significant element in the remit of the four regional Directorates of Health and Social Care. It is also likely that pressure to trial children's services in an integrated and dedicated structure, like a care trust, will intensify following the forthcoming report from the Laming enquiry.

Primary care trusts

Whether or until care trusts become mainstream, NHS/social care interface problems will focus on the relationship with the new Primary

Care Trusts (PCTs). These have taken over community health services (including some community hospitals) which were formerly in NHS trusts, together with other functions from health authorities (now abolished) such as prevention, health promotion and public health. It is questionable whether PCTs which are primarily a vehicle for providing primary care are appropriate bodies to take so much responsibility for the local health economy. If, as current policy intends, they progress towards care trust status they will also take charge of social care.

In his political history of the NHS, Charles Webster suggests that PCTs, currently the 'favoured child of the system' might extend their collaboration with local authorities to 'absorb functions currently within the orbit of social services departments' (Webster 2002).

Webster also points out that PCTs have eclipsed the Personal Medical Services scheme set up in 1997, which, as an alternative method of commissioning, offered a different way forward, using directly employed doctors and other health and social care professionals in a range of local initiatives.

PCTs have effectively replaced health authorities which were responsible for commissioning services. Their establishment has finally jettisoned the purchaser-provider split which clearly distinguished the commissioning function from the providing function in the health service. The development of a 'health market' in the early 1990s allowed for the possibility that purchasing or commissioning of primary care could, in theory, be shared with local authorities offering real accountability and genuine partnership (Cooper *et al*, 1995). Under PCT arrangements, the commissioning of primary and secondary care rests with the providers of primary care.

Local strategic partnerships

Recent government guidance recommends Local Strategic Partnerships (the mechanism for producing community strategies) set up a Children and Young Persons Strategic Partnership as a subset. CYPSPs will set priorities and monitor progress towards agreed targets. Other government guidance on child protection emphasises the importance of partnerships across the community. This sets a foundation for creating new types of integrated services to children and their families and it has been suggested that the CYPSP model could ultimately extend to take on full responsibility for commissioning child care services, whether or not the partnership status was that of a virtual organisation

A similar approach has already been used in the US, where partnerships have been successful in communities of about 20,000 people (too small for PCTs but suited to neighbourhoods). The US experience suggests that focusing on communities and families, as well as on the individual, has been a key factor in making a difference to children's lives (LGA *et al* 2002).

In this country, it might be feasible to reconfigure children's services and education services on the basis of school catchment areas. A joint commissioning model could use pooled budgets and work within the National Strategy for Children which is currently under preparation and may specify aims and outcomes for all children and allow local freedoms to deliver them. Ultimately other services could be organised within the aegis of the Local Strategic Partnership. Alternatively, the LSP it may become a rather nebulous construct, which without a clear function and in the absence of a dedicated budget or team, simply withers on the vine.

Functional agencies

A commonly used alternative to the local government setting, national agencies are functionally based with a separate network for implementation and their own management and chain of command to a government department. Accountability is provided through a minister to Parliament. The probation service is a long-standing example. Many social policies initiated by the present government have relied on functional agencies for their implementation, for example Sure Start, Youth Offending Teams and the Connexions service. It is assumed, rightly or wrongly, that what they lack in local accountability they compensate for in effectiveness, providing focus on a limited range of objectives, often with short term funding and using multi-disciplinary teams.

However, carving up responsibilities in this way has implications for existing organisations. As well as losing staff to the new agencies, existing services also have to address a new set of boundaries, and may need to pick up responsibility at the margins. Functional agencies are sometimes able to achieve their goals by virtue of the fact that other services – such as social services departments – are there to deal with more problematic cases.

It has recently been suggested that creating a more narrowly defined agency to deal solely with child protection would help remove confusion in attitudes towards social workers where parents may be unclear whether social services are investigating them or supporting them. This, it is claimed, would ultimately be of benefit to social services departments who would no longer have to patrol the difficult boundary between care and control. The agency could also provide an appropriate setting for multi-disciplinary work, involving social services, the courts, the police, the probation service, youth work and schools.

However, there is considerable anxiety amongst many people working in social care about removing child protection from local government and handing it to a new justice-based organisation. It is a persuasive argument that children's needs are best addressed in the context of their family, their school and community and that a separate child protection service would make matters worse by creating another set of boundaries across which professionals have to work. Even if a separate agency handled investigation responsibility and registration of children at risk, social services departments would continue to be the key agency in delivering on-going services to child and family.

Other ways of joining up children's services which are being developed at the local level may provide an alternative way forward. Hertfordshire County Council, for example, has amalgamated its Education Department with Social Services, to form a Children Schools and Families Department. All children's services, including child protection, have been merged with education, the youth offending team and youth services, all of whom work to a unified management. The model of accountability adopted by the council – for both users and the public – is one prescribed by the Social Services Inspectorate (Department of Health 2000).

Evolving models of partnership

Since the present government came to power in 1997 the pace of reform in local government and the public sector has been intense. New initiatives have been introduced to tackle poverty and social exclusion, regenerate neighbourhoods and build sustainable communities. Social care has been implicated in all of these, and has also been involved in two major reforms of the NHS. Social care inspection is also undergoing root and branch reform: the National Care Standards Commission lasted less than a month before being replaced. Both health and social care services are seriously fatigued by structural change.

This is not an argument for the status quo but for a period of consolidation and an evolutionary approach to the development of any new structures. Health Act flexibilities offer a range of new partnership arrangements to enable co-operation between local government and the NHS on equal terms. These include pooled budgets, the delegation of functions, lead commissioning and integrated provision. All health-related local authority functions can be included as well as social care. Use of the flexibilities also enables local priorities and objectives identified in the Community Plan and Health Improvement Programmes to be pursued.

Notifications made to the Health and Social Care Joint Unit at the Department of Health show widespread use of Health Act flexibilities, mainly in relation to services for older people, adults with learning difficulties and mental health. Relatively few have been applied to children's services, although there are some exceptions. For example, Wigan has pooled budgets between education, social services and health to set up a multi-professional early intervention team for children's mental health and emotional behavioural development.

In addition to these flexibilities, a range of other initiatives are being developed through local initiative. These include the sharing of professional skills through joint appointments and joint post-holding. Directors of Social Services are also Chief Executives of Primary Care Trusts in Barking and Dagenham, Sandwell, and Southwark. Barking and Dagenham are also using Health Act flexibilities to pool budgets. Instead of choosing to form a care trust, they are operating as a virtual organisation in order to preserve accountability through the council. They also plan to appoint a Director of Public Health jointly with the Housing and Environment department of the council.

Another approach involves reconfiguring responsibility between local government departments to deliver a more integrated service. In the case of Hertfordshire, which has already been referred to, there is no longer a social services department. All children's and family support services have merged with education in Children, Schools and Families, and a second new department, Adult Care Services, has responsibility for services for the elderly and physically disabled as well as adults with learning difficulties and adult mental health services.

Other reforms are achieving service integration by bringing together multi-disciplinary teams on one site to deliver a unified service, for example a single assessment service for child protection in Greenwich, set up by social services and staffed by police, nurses, educational psychologists and social workers.

Care Trusts may provide a format for a limited range of social care functions, which relate more to health, but their effectiveness remains unproven and they attenuate accountability through local democracy. More evaluation is needed before further expansion. Government should therefore allow opportunity for innovation to happen on the ground, from the bottom up. Health Act flexibilities could achieve the desired outcome without resorting to care trusts.

Social services departments face pressure for joint working not only from the NHS, but from a wide range of other agencies. Its ability to do this will be impaired if its structure is dictated solely by the demands of the health service. Instead of pressing ahead with the implementation of care trusts, for which there is no evidence, the Department of Health should focus on specifying outcomes, as in national service frameworks, provide an effective regime of inspection to drive improvement, and allow more local freedom to deliver.

The changing political landscape

Over the next twenty years it is likely that more local government boundaries will be redrawn, albeit sporadically. There are several reasons for this: the experience of unitary authorities may demonstrate a case for their expansion; the pressure to rationalise the wide discrepancies in the population size of authorities; the further rationalisation of the two-tier system of 34 county councils and 238 district councils; and the possibility of selective devolution to English regions, which would be accompanied by parallel changes to unitary authorities. Regional chambers are already in place, and nine Government Offices provide outposts for all major government departments, except the Treasury and the Department of Health.

Pressure for regional assemblies remains largely absent in the south east of England, but is persistently strong in the north east, north west and west midlands. The government's white paper on regional government offers the possibility of their selective implementation following a referendum (Department of Transport, Local Government and the Regions 2002).

The case for regional autonomy is supported by the need to alleviate overload at the centre and to introduce an element of accountability to the considerable amount of governmental and quasi-governmental activity already happening at the regional level. Both arguments are relevant to the NHS, and can be reconciled with its objective of moving to a devolved structure within a regulatory framework. Numerous studies and reports have argued for greater devolution of health from the centre to the regional level:

> What is required is a fundamental rethinking of the relationship between central government and the NHS. The answer could lie in a move to regional government, with the NHS being transferred to the control of bodies like the Spanish regions or Swedish county councils. Democratic renewal and devolution offer the potential to prise the NHS out from the grip of government and the hot house atmosphere of Westminster and Whitehall. The price to be paid may be greater local variation and diversity but given that this already exists between the four countries in the UK, surely this is a price worth paying (Smith, Walsh and Hunter 2001).

The proposed regional assemblies would have a strategic role with a focus on economic development, regeneration and sustainability. Social care contributes to policy development and strategy in these areas locally, but is not included in the functions proposed for the assemblies. Neither are health or education. The proposed structure will replicate the powers and functions awarded to the Greater London Authority itself a severely limited form of devolution, based on a weak executive model. Its powers are, with the exception of transport, entirely strategic.

The White Paper proposes that part of a regional assembly's remit will be to join up the work of different regional stakeholders. The proposed assemblies will work closely with regional public health teams (which are already co-located in government offices) and will have a duty to promote the public health of the region, support the development and implementation of a regional health improvement strategy and appoint the regional Director of Public Health. The creation of a regional assembly will also provide an opportunity to scrutinise existing regional activity and organisations in the public sector. It would also generate pressure to make existing regional bureaucratic structures accountable.

There are currently four Regional Directorates of Health and Social Care (which replaced former health regions in April 2002), whose remit in relation to social care is chiefly developmental. They are intended to be an integral part of the Department of Health and contribute to national as well as local agendas; act as a key managerial interface between the Department and the NHS and have overall responsibility for the development of health and social care within their territory, liaising closely with the Chief Operating Officer, the Modernisation Agency, the Social Services Inspectorate, policy leads and others. They also have an important role in gathering intelligence from the field (from the NHS and social care locally, but also from regional and local government) and making it available to support the wider policy and service development activities of the Department of Health.

The Regional Health and Social Care Directorates will also determine what intervention is necessary when the main programmes of support are not succeeding, holding Strategic Health Authorities to account and supporting performance improvement and intervening where necessary. They will work through the Regional Directors of Public Health and have responsibility for ensuring that the broader health and wellbeing agenda is delivered, forging alliances with the Government Offices and regional and local government. According to the Department of Health, Regional Directors 'will ensure that the concept of a single system of health and social care becomes a reality' (Department of Health 2001c). They are thus influential agents in implementing current models of integration.

From a social care perspective there is a compelling logic in the argument for relocating the present Health and Social Care Directorates in multi-functional regional settings, rather than continuing to have them locked into the Department of Health hierarchy, where NHS considerations overshadow all others. At present they are not even coterminous with the nine Government Offices. The four regions currently used by DOH will come under pressure to realign their boundaries with those of the government offices, particularly if Regional Assemblies are set up.

The Social Services Inspectorate has traditionally operated on a regional basis, and recently changed its regional base to that of the Government Offices. It has effectively performance managed social care, a task which in future, will be integrated with the Regional Directorates of the DOH. By 2004, the SSI will be merged with the National Care Standards Commission into an arm's length agency – the Commission for Social Care Inspection. The long-term future for inspection of social care is likely to see it integrated with health care inspection into a unified regime for which the Commission for Healthcare Audit and Inspection (CHAI) is the prototype. Social care inspection will continue to need a regional network.

Theoretically, a situation could emerge wherein accountability lost locally, for example by wholesale expansion of care trusts to commission and provide health and social care, might be compensated by the emergence of new democratic structures regionally. Elected regional assemblies are likely to interest themselves in the findings of an independent social care inspection commission, which will augment their scrutiny function. They will also need to consider the social care implications of their regional strategies. Despite the feeble example of the Greater London Authority, devolution once begun can be progressive in that it generates its own momentum for further empowerment.

Integrated Health and Social Care Commissioning: an alternative scenario for 2020

The Government can either press ahead with integration of health and social care based on structural reform, or it can do more to promote multi-disciplinary working across boundaries without recourse to new structures. At present it appears to favour the first option, but leaves room for the second. Hopefully a compromise will be reached, accountability will not be impaired and the distinctive values and skills embodied in social care will endure.

A more radical alternative to NHS-social care boundary problems would be to integrate health and social care responsibilities in such a way that both can be locally accountable. This would mean accentuating the distinction between commissioning and providing services. The primary care structures presently in use in the NHS work against this possibility, but thinking long-term allows some recourse to the imagination, and a considerable amount of optimism.

In this scenario, it is sometime between the years 2010 and 2020...

- Local government has been revitalised. Elected mayors, cabinet style councils, electoral reform and the drive for active citizenship have revived local democracy and turn out at local elections is over 60 per cent.

- Social care and health services pursue a common goal of wellbeing, for both the individual and the population as a whole. The local community regards wellbeing a core function of its collective endeavour and regularly mandates its representatives to deliver appropriate services on its behalf, holding it accountable when it fails.

- There are no two-tier local authorities, only unitary authorities and a tier of regional government based on nine government regions, some of which have Regional Assemblies.

- Doctors are no longer independent contractors but are directly employed by nine Regional Health and Social Care Authorities. (RHSCAs) They are thus as amenable to health and social care planning as other health and social care professionals.

- Social workers and other care professionals are as well regarded as doctors and nurses. They work together as self-confident equals. There are few staff shortages in the caring professions.

- Local government has, over the intervening years, accumulated a critical mass of health services competence through its experience of partnership working, use of health act flexibilities, joint commissioning, scrutiny of health services, involvement in health improvement programmes, and strategic planning on behalf of the community.

- Local government has responsibility for commissioning primary health and social care.

- Commissioning managers have transferred from the NHS, having been seconded for a successful trial period. The NHS is responsible for providing health services. It no longer commissions primary care services from itself.

- Each local authority has a social care commissioner/director of social care (successor to directors of social services) working jointly with a health care commissioner. They have chief officer status and jointly head a health and social care commissioning department. The budget is by far the biggest in the local authority. Both commissioners/directors contribute to community plans, local strategic partnerships and other strategies, local and regional. Some social workers are involved in commissioning and strategic functions.

- The local authority also has a director of public health to advise the care commissioning department on the health needs of the population.

- Primary Care Trusts have dis-aggregated into smaller provider trusts delivering a range of services – primary medical care, community health services, health promotion and some related social care. They are managed by the NHS at regional level. Most social care is provided by a range of other trusts, both statutory and voluntary bodies. Many are multi-disciplinary. They operate on contracts with the local authority.

- Many local authorities have merged family and children's services with education. This includes child protection. Many have devolved specific responsibilities to provider trusts. Some have been retained within the direct provision of the local authority. Social workers are employed in any of these settings.

- Primary health care trusts commission or make referrals to all secondary services.

- All health provider trusts, primary and secondary/acute and tertiary/specialist are employed and performance managed by the Regional Health and Social Care Authorities (RHSCAs). They account upwards to the Department of Health and Social Care (DOHSC) and are open to scrutiny by elected Regional Assemblies which have appointment powers to the RHSCA. They also contribute to any regional strategies.

- A parallel health and social care inspection regime based on the nine regions is run by an independent national body, the

Commission for Health and Social Care Audit and Inspection (the successor to CHAI). This inspection body reports to the Department of Health and Social Care and the Department for Local Government.

- Social workers operate in all these settings. It might be as part of their training, on secondments and gaining experience in the voluntary and statutory sectors, in commissioning and providing services, as case workers, in child protection, and in community development.

Conclusion

Central accountability remains integral in a system of publicly funded social care. Effective regulation through inspection can ensure the use of public funds is held accountable to both central government and the taxpayer. Regulation is also instrumental in driving up standards and could provide a framework for ensuring both effective user involvement and public accountability.

Local democratic accountability is essential to encourage public support and community engagement in social care and to ensure responsive services which are tailored to local needs. Whilst user accountability in any public service is vital, it must be additional to public accountability, rather than a substitute for it.

Social care, which aims to achieve the wellbeing of the individual within the community, is a core responsibility of local government. It would be a mistake for the needs of the NHS to dictate the structures used in social care, although they provide a strong impetus. Partnership working is required with a whole range of agencies, particularly services for children where links with education and other family services are important.

Care trusts will take responsibility for social care out of local government into the NHS, a structure which is already heavily centralised with no local democratic accountability.

Where social care needs to integrate more closely with health this could be achieved through commissioning both services within a local government framework. Alternatives to care trusts are already developing through local initiative in ways which ensure local accountability and responsiveness to local circumstances. Social care is being delivered by multi-professional teams in various inter-agency settings now evolving in local government. Integrating processes, such as assessment and referrals and building services around the user are the kinds of structural change most likely to be of benefit.

Important questions remain about the optimum scale for the delivery of services. The current organisation of local government is such that social services departments are serving very different population sizes. Rationalisation may come with the introduction of regional assemblies, which could be accompanied by the removal of two tier authorities and their replacement by unitary authorities. Regional structures within the NHS are not coterminous with regional government offices and may also require rationalisation in future. However, further work is needed to identify the implications, and potential opportunities, of any such reforms.

Finally, policy makers need to acknowledge that structural reform does not provide a panacea. Social care, like health and education has been in a state of structural upheaval for the past decade and longer. Further reform of the structures that deliver social care is less important than the need to develop a skilled workforce and increase capacity.

Bibliography

CIPFA (1998) *Accountability: a framework for public services*

Cooper L, Coote A, Davies A and Jackson C (1995) *Voices Off: tackling the democratic deficit in health* London: IPPR

Department of Health (2001a) *Involving Patients and the Public in Healthcare: a Discussion Document* London: The Stationery Office

Department of Health (2001b) *Modern Social Services – a commitment to deliver* The 10th Annual Report of the Chief Inspector of Social Services 2000-2001 London: The Stationery Office Office

Department of Health (2001c) *Shifting the Balance of Power within the NHS: Securing Delivery*

Department of Health (2000) *Quality Strategy for Social Care, Consultation Document* London: The Stationery Office

Department of Health (1998) *Modernising Social Services* London: The Stationery Office

Department of Transport, Local Government and the Regions (2002) *Your Region Your Choice: revitalising the English regions* London: The Stationery Office

The Guardian (2002) Quoted in 'Milburn: Cash Boost Depends on Joint Working' *The Guardian* 13 March 2002

The Guardian (2001a) 'Bill at Breaking Point – LGA and Ministers in rift over care trust proposals' *The Guardian* 4 April 2001

The Guardian (2001b) 'Only Fools and Trojan Horses' *The Guardian* 14 February 2001

King's Fund (2001) *Future Imperfect: Report of the Kings Fund Care and Support Inquiry* London: The Kings Fund

LGA, NHS Confederation and Association of Directors of Social Services (2002) *Serving Children Well: a new vision for children's services* London: Local Government Association

Peck E *et al* (2002) 'Going Halves' *Health Services Journal* 18 April 2002

Peck E, Towell D, and Gulliver P (2001) 'The Meanings of Culture in Health and Social Care: a study of the combined Trust in Somerset' *Journal of Interprofessional Care* 2001 15.4

Smith J, Walsh K and Hunter D (2001) 'The 'Re-disorganisation of the NHS' *BMJ* 2001; 323

Stewart J and Stoker G (1988) *From Local Administration to Community Government* Fabian Research Series 351, The Fabian Society

Stoker G and Travers T (2001) *A New Account? Choices in Local Government Finance* Joseph Rowntree Foundation

Webster C (2002) *The National Health Service: A Political History* OUP

Wistow G (2001) 'Modernisation, the NHS Plan and Healthy Communities' *Journal of Management in Medicine* 15.5